A Companion on the South Downs Way

G000270420

An Idiosyncratic Look

with

Peter Anderson

on the keyboards

and

Terry Owen

behind the camera

"I encountered Mr Hackman, an Englishman, who has been walking the length and breadth of Europe for several years. I enquired of him what were his chief observations. He replied gruffly, 'I never look up' and went on his way."

N Brooke MD 1796
Quoted in **The Vintage book of Walking (2000)**

"'Curiouser and curiouser!' cried Alice"

Alice's Adventures in Wonderland
Lewis Carroll

Also by Peter Anderson and Terry Owen: **Tandridge Border Path**
Sussex Ouse Valley Way

To our wives, Jayne and Cathy, for all their support throughout but who were secretly grateful that it got us out from under their feet whilst relieved that we were saved from hanging around street corners.

And the critic said: *"You two think you're normal"* Cathy Owen, 17 May 2003

The right of Peter Anderson to be identified as the author of this work is hereby asserted pursuant to the Copyright, Design and Patents Act 1988.

Designed by *IntegrityDesignandPrint@hotmail.co.uk*

Printed by Hastings Printing Company Limited

First published by Per-Rambulations in 2006

Per-Rambulations

Larkshill, Cranston Road, East Grinstead, West Sussex, RH19 3HL.
Tel: 01342 315786
www.per-rambulations.co.uk

Contents

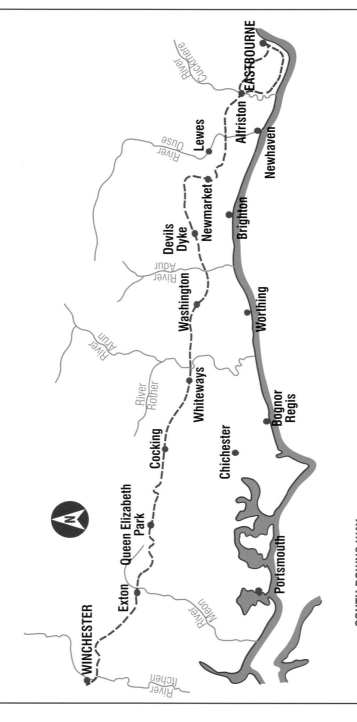

- - - - - SOUTH DOWNS WAY

Foreword

The South Downs are one of the best known and loved hill ranges in the world and they are a procreative force that renews itself from generation to generation but they have not hitherto produced a book quite like this one. The object of the author and the photographer is quite simple – to help us to indulge in the pleasure of setting out on foot on the long distance path between Eastbourne and Winchester known as the South Downs Way. That supreme Sussex walker, S P B Mais, has written of walking as the *"healthiest and cheapest exercise and the purest of human pleasures. Few things have added so much to the sum of human happiness as walking."* This book makes one impatiently want to set off for the billows of the Downs but what makes it different from others written on the Downs is its companionableness – it is so rightly called a 'companion'. Like any good human companion on a pleasurable walk the book wears its learning lightly yet tries to answer the questions that a newcomer to the chalk hills is likely to raise. It shows how easily you can find quietude and loveliness on the Downs.

Whether it is a still morning with no cloud in the sky and the sea a soft deep blue; a blustery autumn day in the teeth of a strong south-westerly (Belloc's weather); or, dare I mention it? – the discomfort of wet clothes and squealing boots in December until warmed by the fireside of a village inn – the book offers an insight into the complete and credible alternative world to the suburb, town and city that is the well – beloved Downs and involves no road-walking.

A good feature of the book is chapters which deal with each stage in the annual South Downs Way Walk. The maximum of enjoyment can be obtained from a walk of some 8-12 miles which is roughly the length of each section. A day's journey of this kind by the footslogger in the cream of south country walking allows for the reading of the 'Companion', loitering to hear birdsong, picking berries and wild mushrooms in autumn, contemplating the harvest scene and calling in at the humble parish churches within sight of the Way in the National Park to be. Best of all, for since the end of food shortages we have not had to take our rations with us, this allows time to be genial in the nearby village inn. Each of these sections, as the book points out, has its own agreeably varied characteristics and its own places acquired for us by the National Trust.

So let the 'Companion' show you where to walk, what to see and how to learn about the Downs. You will return the better for the sudden elation to feel the immensity of the sky above your head and for knowing about Gilbert White's mountains, prehistoric barrows, smuggling yarns, legends, place-names, writers and a host of other things. Then you will have captured something of what Arthur Beckett, the first president of the Society of Sussex Downsmen (now the South Downs Society) called the "*spirit of the Downs*". In the unlikely event that ninety-nine of your enquiries lead to nowhere you may be inspired to write a 'Companion' of your own!

Dr Peter Brandon

Author of 'The South Downs'
President of the South Downs Society

Before We Start

"Another book on the South Downs? Aren't there quite a lot already?"

Over the years there have been many books on the South Downs and the South Downs Way, but many are not now in print and none, hopefully, are quite like this one.

Although I have been fortunate to live in sight of the South Downs for more than thirty years and to have walked on them for longer, it was not until 2001 that I realised just how little I really knew about the Downs and what could be seen from the South Downs Way. I had became part of the team escorting the annual South Downs Way Walk that is promoted by the West Sussex County Council and now organised by Footprints of Sussex. I found that I could not answer many of the questions that either I asked myself or my fellow walkers were asking me.

Notes were prepared for the team. Those notes are here much expanded into a book but that book is not and never was intended to be a guide to the South Downs Way. It has only one general map and few route directions, and those only if there is need to take care in following the Way or that a diversion from the official route might not be inappropriate. It is intended that it should supplement the route guides that are necessarily constrained by space: to answer some of your questions: some of which, perhaps, you did not know that you even wanted to ask. Neither the guide books nor good maps should be neglected.

Expanding the notes into a book was not just a way of showing off or, indeed, of creating a reminder for me at a time when my short term memory seems to be becoming more erratic than it used to be. I feel that the more that one knows about a place, however little, the more a sense of belonging is fostered: ownership in that modern sense of adopting or accepting ideas rather than physical ownership: of belonging to place not of place belonging to someone.

Perceptions of the countryside have also changed. Not all that long ago the rural predominated over the urban. Now the roles are reversed. Most people no longer have any links with the countryside. Some regard it as something preserved in aspic, or on a pretty picture, forever unchanging with no past or future, not a place with a continuous history where people have lived and worked for thousands of years and continue to live and work. There are no smells: no mud: no discomfort or inconvenience. But the reverse is true. The countryside is real and living and the South Downs are part of that living reality.

It may be in that in trying to approach those who have lived along and within sight of the Way this book has become people and place oriented at the neglect of geology and natural history. How the Downs were formed will, however, be found in the published guides and I am anxious not to go over anything that they have covered unless there is something new or more to be said. Little too has been said about the wildlife for much the same reason; others have written far more knowledgeably and better than I am able.

An index is also missing. It was not overlooked. A good index is a matter of art or science: perhaps a mixture of both. A bad index is a loathsome thing. It is better to have none at all especially as it is hoped that you will read the appropriate section of this book either just before, or just after tackling a stage, or even carry it with you as you go. The main hope, however, is that you will enjoy reading it.

The major theme is the South Downs Way: what lies along it and what can be seen on it or from it without straying too far off it; and although the temptation to look over the hill was usually severely resisted, it was sometimes too strong.

The Way is one of the 15 National Trails in England and Wales. It was officially opened on 15 July 1972 when it then terminated at the border with Hampshire. It was not the first of the National Trails. That honour belongs to the Pennine Way officially opened in 1965. It was, however, the first long distance bridleway. It lies wholly within two Areas of Outstanding Natural Beauty (AONB), the Sussex Downs AONB and the East Hampshire AONB and, as an added bonus, the first stages out of Eastbourne are along a Heritage Coast. It may soon run through a newly created South Downs National Park.

The annual South Downs Way Walk starts at Eastbourne and Winchester in alternate years. It is purely accidental that the start was in Eastbourne in the year that the notes, the foundation for this book, were first prepared and that became the direction followed here. The stages here are also those that are used for the annual walk and are the logical stages if the Way is tackled in a series of linear sections.

Opinions are divided over which is the best direction to walk the Way. Whether it is better to start in Winchester and apparently climb slowly and steadily to the heights of the Seven Sisters and Beachy Head with its commanding position over the finish at Eastbourne: or to start at Eastbourne and, after the resounding start along the cliffs, head towards a more gentle finish going down to the ancient capital of England. For some a deciding factor is that in the south of England the weather usually comes from the west. A Winchester start puts most of the wind and rain at your back instead of having to face into it. Either way gives different perspectives. There is always a sense of achievement whichever direction is followed.

If there is a message it is that continual vigilance is needed to protect the Downs, and they do need protection. They cannot be preserved in some unchanging form for change affects everything but, without care, much can disappear never to be recovered especially that tranquillity that still remains in spite of many inroads. Writing in 1900, W H Hudson (**Nature in Downland**) saw the forces of change at work when he wrote of the passing of the slow, patient ox teams but he did not see how far that change would go:
"The little rustic village in the deep dene, with its two or three hundred inhabitants, will probably outlast London, or at all events London's greatness; and the solitary shepherd with his dog at his feet will doubtless stand watching his flock on the hillside for some thousands of years to come; …"

Irrevocable changes have occurred in little much more than a century, a moment in the time scale of the Downs, but pressure for change accelerated. Fortunately the Downs have their guardians like the South Downs Society that since its foundation in 1923 has been instrumental in preserving that which otherwise would have been lost, and without which racing cars might have roared along the crest of the Downs and housing estates proliferated. The Society will no doubt forgive me if I say that new members are always welcome.

Finally, a caveat: at all times of the year there can be stunning days on the Downs that are so bright and clear that you can almost see forever. It is hoped that these are the ones that you encounter. It is not always so. It is not quite as bad as if you can see the Downs, it is going to rain and, if you cannot see the Downs, it is raining but there are those times when the weather closes in, the long views disappear, the familiar become the unfamiliar and the compass essential.

And do take heed of the walking guidebooks and wear and carry what they advise.   Peter Anderson, May 2006

Some High Spots along and by the Way

Heights given in the books sometimes differ from each other and also from those given on the Ordnance Survey maps. The following heights are taken from the Ordnance Survey Maps and have been converted into feet by multiplying by 3.2808. This will account for the Imperial measurement differing marginally from that given in some of the older texts.

Although Gilbert White, the 18th century naturalist, did describe them as *"the vast range of mountains called the Sussex-downs..."*, none of the hills meets even the old fashioned definition of a mountain at 1,000 feet but the Downs are nevertheless impressive seen from afar or from the foot of the escarpment.

The highest point on the South Downs is Butser Hill in Hampshire not far from the border between Hampshire and West Sussex at 270 metres (889 feet). The highest point on the Sussex Downs is Crown Tegleaze (Littleton Down) near Duncton at 253 metres (830 feet).

Heights on or close to the Way from east to west in sequence include:
- Beachy Head . . . . 164 m (538 ft)
- Windover Hill where the Long Man lurks . . . . 188 m (617 ft)
- Firle Beacon. . . . . 217 m (712 ft)
- Beddingham Hill * . . . . 189 m (620 ft)
- Itford Hill. . . . . 164 m (538 ft)
- Blackcap . . . . 206 m (676 ft)
- Ditchling Beacon . . . . 248 m (814 ft)
- Keymer Post. . . . . 234 m (768 ft)
- Wolstonbury Hill. . . . . 206 m (676 ft)
- Dyke Hill. . . . . 217 m (712 ft) (at trig. point)
- Truleigh Hill * . . . . 216 m (709 ft)
- Chanctonbury Hill . . . . 238 m (781 ft)
- Rackham Hill . . . . 193 m (633 ft)
- Bignor Hill . . . . 225 m (738 ft)
- Gatting Beacon * (near Bignor Hill). . . . . 245 m (804 ft)
- Crown Tegleaze . . . . 253 m (830 ft)
- Linch Down near Cocking . . . . 248 m (814 ft)
- Beacon Hill, Harting . . . . 242 m (794 ft)
- Butser Hill * . . . . 270 m (886 ft)
- Old Winchester Hill . . . . 197 m (646 ft)
- Beacon Hill above Exton . . . . 201 m (659 ft)
- Cheesefoot Head. . . . . 176 m (577 ft)

* These hills have radio masts on them which makes them easier to identify from a distance

The heights above are at the summits of the hills and the Way does not always reach that high. Although Butser Hill is the highest point on the South Downs, the Way itself crosses a shoulder of the hill at a maximum height of 245 metres. The answer to the question, what is the highest that the Way itself reaches, could well be a draw at 245 metres between Butser Hull and Ditchling Beacon. Although Ditchling Beacon is 248 metres, the Way passes just under that height. The summit of Linch Down is also 248 metres but the Way at that point does not go above 236 metres. The Way is at 234 metres as it passes Crown Tegleaze the highest point on the Sussex Downs.

But how long is it?

Although there appears to be some disagreement in some of the guidebooks, the Countryside Agency, which is responsible for the National Trails in England, puts the official starting and ending points at the western end of Eastbourne promenade and at the City Mill, where the river Itchen flows underneath the High Street, in Winchester. The Agency also says that it is 160 kilometres (100 miles) long. The Agency does, however, caution that it should be remembered *"…that the distances you walk will always be greater than the mapped distance due to climbs and descents of hills you will encounter along the route"*.

The Way is also continually evolving. A recent introduction has been an alternative route to pass safely through the village of Washington, and closer to the Frankland Arms. This will add to the distance but avoids an attempt on the dual carriageway of the A24 hurtling towards the South Coast and back again. The solution to more than 20 years uncertainty over the route in Hampshire by rerouting it over the top of Beacon Hill above the Meon Valley will affect the mileage, as could proposals that are under consideration for the last miles into Winchester, one of which would be via St Catherine's Hill.

One's personal mileage will also be lengthened by the method that one walks the Way. If it is by means of a series of linear walks there will be detours to car parks or public transport. If it involves staying along the Way, there will be descents to one's accommodation in the evening and the greater test of regaining the tops the following morning after a full English breakfast.

One thing is for sure. If you start at one end of the South Downs Way and walk to the other, you will break the barrier of a hundred miles.

Eastbourne to Alfriston

"Ah! hills so early loved! in fancy still
I breathe your pure keen air; and still behold
Those widely spreading views, mocking alike
The Poet and the Painters utmost art."

Charlotte Smith *(1749-1806)*
From ***Beachy Head***

There is little to show beyond the information board and the lone fingerpost pointing ahead as you start the climb up to Beachy Head that, leaving the opening tarmac behind, you have set out on foot along the South Downs Way. The path stretches ahead and up. The one consolation is that here it is never as quite as long and steep as one remembers from previous occasions. But it is fair to describe what is to come as the most undulating on the whole of the South Downs Way. It is certainly the most dramatic.

If one pauses on the first steep slope on the cliff route up to Beachy Head to look back to admire the view over Eastbourne – a must for some of us more mature walkers even at this early stage on the journey – the Pevensey Levels beyond Eastbourne can be seen and it is said that sharp eyes (which lets some of us out) can pick out the walls of Pevensey Castle that has served in the defence of England for nearly two thousand years: Roman fort: Norman Castle inside; and Second World War defences built into the foot of the Roman walls. It is also said that it is possible to see as far as Hastings and the Fairlight Cliffs and Dungeness.

You have missed the Way if you see Beachy Head lighthouse from this angle

At the top the octagonal base of what was once the Lloyds Watch Tower stands nearer to the edge. It was in use until 1904 to send back news by semaphore to London of incoming ships: valuable commercial information for the insurance and commodity markets. When that use finished it became a kiosk for the sale of postcards. It fell into disrepair and was given to Eastbourne Council in 1948. The top structure was removed and it became the base for a pay telescope.

One of the plaques mounted on the side of the Tower commemorates PC Harry Ward BEM who is shown mounted on his horse Jumbo. Until his retirement in 1966 PC Ward was one of the mounted Downs Rangers that were for many years provided by the police. The plaque reminds that, *"On numerous occasions he risked his life attempting to save others"*. That, in turn, reminds that Beachy Head is a place where lives are lost both by accident and design: from the top and by the sea below. It also helps to remind of all, whether coastguard, police officer, doctor, member of the ambulance service, helicopter crew, the crew of lifeboats standing offshore below and everybody else who often at the risk of their lives have given, and will continue to give, help, life and hope to those in need.

Rescues are not only of those who have accidentally fallen or jumped but of those who have attempted to climb up or down the cliffs to find too late that it is beyond their competence. There are the dogs too that have been brought back up to the top, at least one of which showed his gratitude by sinking its teeth into its rescuer.

Approximately twenty metres beyond the Watch Tower is another plaque that is set not much more than ankle height above the grass on which there is the 4th verse of the 93rd Psalm:

"Mightier than the thunders of many waters,
Mightier than the waves of the sea,
The Lord on high is mighty."

And below that:

"God is always greater than all of our troubles."
MB

This is one of those small mysteries that occur along the Way. There is

nothing to indicate when, why or by whom it was set up and enquiries have failed to answer these questions. Is it, perhaps, to give pause for thought or in thanksgiving for avoiding what might have happened?

Also beyond the Watch Tower the Way meets the surfaced Peace Path for a while taking in a viewpoint out to sea. The Peace Path was levelled and surfaced in 1987 to celebrate the United Nations International Year of Peace in 1986. The Path runs in a rough semicircle to the south and south east of the Beachy Head Inn and Countryside Centre.

For centuries Beachy Head has had a fearsome reputation among sailors. By the late 1980s over 70 shipwrecks had been recorded, the earliest being the *Marie* from Santander in 1368. There undoubtedly have been many more only evidenced by what is washed ashore with nothing to show from what ship it came.

A gravestone in the churchyard close to the east end of the ancient church at East Dean records the death of Parson Darby on 26th October 1726 and has the inscription, *"He was the sailors' friend"*. He was instrumental in saving the life of many a sailor by what was known as Parson Darby's Hole or Parson Darby's Cave. It was a chimney cut up through the chalk cliff from the beach by the Parson or, possibly, by smugglers and improved by him, although the true origins of the chimney may have been far, far older than any smugglers. Those who had been shipwrecked could climb up the chimney with the assistance of ropes and take shelter in 'rooms' that had also been cut in the chalk. It no longer exists: a victim of cliff falls.

The Parson did hang a light to guide people to the cave and also to warn those at sea of impending danger but there was dire need of a lighthouse.

Squire John Fuller of Brightling in East Sussex (1757-1834) – Mad Jack Fuller – renowned for the follies that he built at Brightling had the gravest of concern for the safety of sailors. In the early 1820s he provided a lifeboat to Eastbourne and later, in 1828, built the first lighthouse, a wooden clad structure, at Belle Tout. By doing so he was principally instrumental in the building of the Belle Tout lighthouse that still stands. Building works on that started in 1832; the light was first lit on 11th October 1834. Incredibly it served until 1902, when it was superseded by the present lighthouse, even though it had the habit of disappearing in the not uncommon cliff top mists.

Like the lighthouse at Belle Tout that it replaced, the present lighthouse at sea level is built from granite blocks. The light is 103 feet (31 metres) above the spring high water mark. It was manned until 1983 when it became fully automated. The original external decor was black and white, the white originally being provided by the natural light colour of the granite. The red and white scheme was introduced in 1951 to assist inshore shipping. The light shows two flashes in quick succession every twenty seconds. There is also a fog horn to sound mournfully through the fog when needed.

Nine nautical miles out to sea from Beachy Head the Royal Sovereign is an offshore shoal that is notorious for shipwrecks. It is now marked by a light-tower 159 feet high described as "*looking like a marine mushroom*" that can be seen on clear days to the south east of Beachy Head. It replaced a lightship in 1971. It was manned until 1994 when it was fully automated. The shoal is named after a ship but opinions differ which one of that name it was.

The yellow concrete markers that are set in the turf after passing Beachy Head and descending into *Shooters' Bottom* are used to measure cliff erosion from aerial photos.

The white cliffs remain white through erosion, otherwise they would disappear under vegetation, but cliff erosion is a never ending danger. There have been substantial falls at Beachy Head in recent years. The gloomy forecast that Belle Tout, which can be seen ahead, will fall into the sea, has been temporarily postponed. In 1999 when it had reached 3 metres from the edge, the entire building was lifted two feet in the air and moved by back 17 metres. It is said that should safeguard it for another two hundred years although there is another school of thought that similar operations might have to be carried out every 20 to 30 years. In 2005 the cliff edge certainly appeared to be perilously close to the approach road to the lighthouse. The lighthouse does, however, seem to be a survivor. It suffered badly in World War II from gunnery practice either through poor aim or bored gunners wanting to do other than fire out to sea. There is a sad photograph showing the results of its war service.

The removal operation was televised: Belle Tout's second major television appearance. Earlier in 1987 it was used as a main setting in the BBC's dramatisation of Fay Weldon's novel *The Life and Loves of a She-Devil*.

It is now a private residence and was on the rental market in 2002. For those who want to upgrade a beach hut, the estimated rent was between £2,500 and £3000 per calendar month. Although with the prices that have been reported of late for some beach huts, there may not be all that much of a uplift.

It has been said that 'Belle Tout' does not come from the French meaning everything is lovely but that the 'Tout' (pronounced toot) is a corruption of an Old English word meaning look-out and the 'Belle' is apparently the name of an ancient god. The volume for Sussex in the monumental series published by the English Place Names Society states that the first recorded use of the name was in 1724 as 'Beltout' without further explanation, so it may be a comment on the view after all. And 'Beachy Head' has nothing to do with beaches. It is another corruption; this time certainly from French. The 'Beachy' comes from *beau chef* meaning beautiful headland. The 'Head' is superfluous and was added later when the original meaning had been forgotten.

Everybody must know of the opening to Kipling's *A Smuggler's Song*:

> *"If you wake at midnight, and hear a horse's feet,*
> *Don't go drawing back the blind, or looking in the street,*
> *Them that asks no questions isn't told a lie.*
> *Watch the wall, my darling, while the Gentlemen go by!*
> *Five and twenty ponies*
> *Trotting through the dark -*
> *Brandy for the Parson,*
> *'Baccy for the Clerk:*
> *Laces for a Lady, letters for a spy,*
> *And watch the wall, my darling, while the gentlemen go by."*

It has been said that in its heyday smuggling was the second largest industry in south east England after agriculture: so almost the whole of the south east coast was smuggling territory. The section of the South Downs Way between Eastbourne and Beachy Head is the closest that the South Downs Way comes to the coast and favoured landing spots such as Birling Gap and Cuckmere Haven.

The River Cuckmere, like the Ouse which the Way crosses at Southease Bridge, provided a very convenient route inland. It is also no coincidence that watch houses and cottages, still standing apart from those lost to the sea through erosion, were built for the Coast Blockade at Birling Gap and Cuckmere Haven and that HMS Congo was moored in Cuckmere Haven from 1819 to 1825 when the building works were completed. The Coast Blockade was formed in 1817 when the war against smuggling was stepped up, the Royal Navy having the capacity for it when ships and men became available following the end of the Napoleonic Wars.

HMS Congo was a paddle schooner built at Deptford in 1816. She was never used under steam and her engine was removed in 1818. She was called Congo because she was originally built to survey the river Congo. She was not a success as she was too big to get very far up river. Government contracts do not seem to have improved very much; Millennium Domes and bridges seem to be cast in the same mould.

Kipling's caravan of five and twenty must have been taken from when smuggling was in decline. At the height men and horses were numbered in the hundreds and, although some of the men involved might have been from the gentry, smugglers were not as a rule gentlemen, whether nature's or otherwise: far from it: murder, terror tactics and public displays of force and violence were not uncommon. And everybody, or almost everybody, was at it. It is said that in the late 18th century on the Stanmer estate (now mainly covered by the University of Sussex) only the owner, Henry Pelham, was not involved. An estate bailiff was an organiser and the chaplain was injured returning from a run at Rottingdean. Comments, politically correct or otherwise, about the present student population at Stanmer and smuggling, lawlessness or any other ageist diatribe are left to the individual.

Smuggling in England did not start with goods in but, from medieval times onwards, with goods out: mainly wool on which the then prosperity of England rested but fullers' earth, used in the processing of wool, was also involved. And Kipling left out the most popular and lucrative import – tea; but it does not scan, the bottom dropped out of that market overnight when the import duty was slashed and it is not so romantic as the other things on Kipling's list.

Birling Gap below Belle Tout has been under attack on two fronts: erosion by the sea and housing development, the sea being the more successful. Old photographs show the cliff face used to extend well beyond the row of coastguard cottages the end of which has now been claimed by the sea. On the other front ambitions were nursed over a long period between 1885 and 1930 to develop housing at Birling Gap. These fortunately came to nothing. Fortunate for those who walk there and, perhaps, for the householders who might have seen their homes also disappear into the sea.

Beyond Birling Gap, one traverses the undulations of the Seven Sisters themselves although it is said that there is an eighth uncounted sister.

From east to west the Sisters are:

- Went Hill Brow at 45 metres (146 feet)
- Baily's Brow at 60 metres (194 feet)
- Flagstaff Point at 47 metres (153 feet)
- Brass Point at 50 metres (160 feet)
- Rough Brow at 67 metres (276 feet)
- Short Brow at 66 metres (214 feet)
  – and finally the highest, and sometimes it feels like it,
- Haven Brow at 78 metres (253 feet)

The unregarded 'eighth' sister is Flat Brow. She lies between Baileys Brow and Flagstaff Point.

In Michel Dean, the valley between the first and second sisters, one passes the obelisk marking the gift of the land at Michel Dean to the National Trust by Mr W A Robertson in memory to his two brothers who were killed in the first World War. This echoes another memorial in Surrey of a similar gift to the National Trust by the same gentleman also in memory of his brothers. That was of Highcomb Copse at the Devil's Punch Bowl. The National Trust now owns the whole of the Punch Bowl and another irreplaceable area has also been preserved.

There is another memorial further along at Flagstaff Point. Although it has its place in the guides, it would be churlish not to mention it again. It is to celebrate the donation of £5,000 made by William Campbell in 1926 that completed the appeal for £17,000 launched by the Society of Sussex Downsmen that enabled them to buy the Crowlink Valley to safeguard it from building development. In 2005 at the request of the National Trust the seat around the monument was installed by the Society to replace a seat that had been nearby until demolished due to its closeness of the edge of the cliff.

More than seven sisters

The purposely transient also sometimes finds a place on the clifftop. In August 2005 a piece of environmental art created to reflect its surroundings appeared above Birling Gap. Made from woven greenwood and chalk daub, **Vanishing Point** was to epitomize the unceasing erosion of the landscape. For a while it engaged the distant attention of some of the cattle illustrated above.

The Way descends from the Seven Sisters into the Cuckmere Estuary. The meanders marking the course of the river before it was channelled can clearly be seen and are world famous. What may not be appreciated is that this is another landscape that is under threat; sea levels are rising, climate change, for whatever reason, is producing increasingly stormy weather and the flood banks along the present course of the river are starting to collapse. A 'managed retreat' is planned: to work with rather than against nature. Flood defence would be provided by restoring the natural estuary. The meanders would flow again and the surrounding flood plain would be recreated. This would provide not only flood defence but also add to the nationally diminishing habitats of salt marsh and mudflats and so increase the diversity of wildlife.

Threats here are not only by the sea but also from the sea. Although the last successful foreign invasion of Britain was over a thousand years ago in 1066 by William of Normandy, now known as the Conqueror, there have been raids from across the Channel and fears of invasion ever since, as shown by the defences from all ages that can be seen along the south coast. The Victorians were still building defences against a French invasion even though Napoleon was gone: Newhaven Fort just along the coast was originally constructed in the 1860s for that reason. Later came defences in the two World Wars.

These produced the small defence posts known as pill boxes. If one continues towards Exceat along the concrete road instead of following the South Downs Way over the shoulder of the hill, one passes beneath an uncommon round pill box dating from the first World War (1914-1918).

The Way passes the visitor centre at Exceat. Those who are aficionados of cream teas should be able to satisfy their hunger at the cafe in the old farm house. The farm used oxen for ploughing as late as 1926. At that time it would not have been the red coated Sussex Cattle. They had fallen into disfavour and been largely replaced by black Welsh oxen that were thought to be stronger and hardier.

The village of Exceat once lay on the south side of the main road. It is said to have been wiped out as a result of the Black Death in 1349 but although the Black Death is often quoted as the reason for a village being deserted the truth may be otherwise. The village still existed in 1460 over a hundred years after the Black Death although by then only two houses still stood and the church was ruined. The frequent and ferocious French raids in the late fourteenth century that savaged the area may be a more likely explanation for the decline of the village leading to its eventual disappearance. The site of the church has been discovered and is marked by a stone on the hillside above the Way.

There is a green telephone box standing at the entrance to the car park opposite the visitor centre at Exceat and another near the foot of the long set of steps leading down to the village of Westdean. It was felt that nothing would be easier than finding out why they were painted green. This was not to be the case. The writers of the books consulted appeared not to have noticed; those in the locality either accepted them as a fact of life or had varying theories. In the absence of an official explanation from BT the most likely explanation is so that they will blend into the countryside. For this reason public telephone boxes are painted green or grey in some National Parks. But a further mystery remains. The back of the telephone box opposite the Visitor Centre is painted red. A logical explanation is to make it conspicuous to anybody needing to summon help after encountering difficulties along the estuary or on the beach. There is one flaw in the argument. There is currently no telephone inside.

The Long Man of Wilmington is not the only chalk figure in the neighbourhood. As you go up what is the last ascent before Alfriston, keep an eye out over your left shoulder. You should see the Litlington Horse on the hillside across the Cuckmere Valley. The present horse is 90 feet long and is a mere youngster cut in 1925. It replaced an earlier horse there that appeared in 1838, Queen Victoria's Coronation Year. It is said that the original horse commemorates a young girl killed when thrown from her horse bolting downhill. It is also said that the original horse was cut in one day by a local man, Mr J. Pagden of Frog Firle, and his brothers.

On the last stage into Alfriston, along by the river Cuckmere, the thatched roofed Clergy House lies ahead. As most know, it was the first house to be bought by the then newly formed National Trust in 1896 for the price of £10. Beyond that lies the 14th century Parish Church of Alfriston. It is dedicated to St Andrew and sometimes called the Cathedral of the South Downs. It is unusual in its cruciform shape, each arm of the 'cross' being of equal length. There is a similar church at Poynings that lies close to the Devil's Dyke.

Like many another old church the church is built on a mound. A church built on a mound is often an indication that that was a spot where older religions were practised before conversion to Christianity. It may have been for that reason that it was first planned to build the church on another site in a field to the west of the village street; but every time building was started the stones were whirled up in the night and flung onto the mound where the church now stands. Nobody knew what to do until one day four oxen were found lying on the mound, their rumps touching, in the form of a cross with equal arms, and that is how and where the church was built and where it now stands.

Until at least the 1930s, and it is said that the last recorded case was at Alfriston in 1935, and possibly later, shepherds were been buried with a lock of wool in their hands so that St Peter might see that they were shepherds and allow them into Heaven in spite of the many times that tending their flocks had made them miss church on a Sunday.

There is also a South Downs bridleway that runs from Eastbourne to Winchester and, for the most part, it follows the same route as the footpath. From Eastbourne, however, the bridleway runs inland to Alfriston and does not take the cliff path. It passes through Jevington, one of whose claims to fame is as the birthplace of Banoffee Pie at a restaurant called The Hungry Monk, before passing above the head of the Long Man of Wilmington, the tallest chalk figure in Britain, and circling down into Alfriston.

The Long Man cannot actually be seen from the Way but those who know him or have seen pictures of him with what appear to be a staff in each hand will realise that he has an uncanny resemblance to a modern walker using two walking poles: perhaps a prophetic vision by the monks who were thought to have carved him or a representation of a visitor from space demonstrating an advanced walking technique. A further deduction from his rather obvious missing point of difference from the Cerne Abbas giant could be that he was the creation of an early feminist movement.

Recent research, alas, suggests that the Long Man may not be as mature as we might like to suppose: only in or about the 17th century: a mere stripling at 400 years or so.

The Long Man enjoys a rare distinction. His picture appears on the Ordnance Survey map. He can be found in situ on the side of Windover Hill on the 1:25,000 scale OS Explorer 123. A magnifying glass may help.

Alfriston to the A27

"And if you climb up old Caburn to view the Celtic Camp,
And look across the Wealden plain when mists rise thick and damp,
You'll see about the foot o' Firle the Romans' brave array,
Or Saxon soldiers coming home at purple close o' day."

Arthur Beckett (1871-1943)
First President of the Society of Sussex Downsmen
(now the South Downs Society)
From **Downland**

The trouble with Alfriston is, like so many other places in Sussex, the pronunciation of the name. It is spelt ALFriston but some of the books hold that it is pronounced ORLEfriston. And that is without going into whether the stress is on the first syllable, on the last friston or riston, or equal stress on both. Some hold that it is ALF as it was the town of King Alfred the Great and that the name means Alfred's town. The name really means that it was the farmstead or tun of a Saxon called Ælfric who received his land from Alfred the Great in return for military service.

Alfred did have a palace close by at Westdean (sometimes rendered West Dean) the village tucked away at the bottom of the long flight of steps down through the woods shortly after the climb up from the Visitor Centre at Exceat. There is also a local tradition that Alfriston was where Alfred burnt the cakes and the Star Inn, certainly at one time, displayed an iron pot claimed to be the very one used by King Alfred on that occasion. It may still do so.

But going back to pronunciation: Hilaire Belloc, and we shall be meeting him more than once on the Way, had strong views on a great many things including the pronunciation of Sussex names. It all arose from when Adam (assisted by Eve) came to name all the places on earth and desired to especially distinguish Sussex which he did by making "*her names of a sort that should give fools to think*". Part of that was that 'th', 'ph' and 'sh' should not be pronounced as a single sound "*under pain of damnation*": thus, Bos-ham, Felp-ham and, according to Belloc, Hors-ham, which has to do with a town with a connection with horses and not from any other form of human activity.

Alfriston is still well in smuggling country. Close to the market cross is the Smugglers' Inn. It used to be called Market Cross House and was the home of Stanton Collins, a butcher, who was the 'Mr Big' of smuggling in the area in the 1820s. That he and his men had influence is shown when they were called in to settle a dispute over the rightful preacher at what is now the United Reform Church. He was never convicted of smuggling. That may also testify to his influence but, in 1831, he was sentenced to seven years transportation for stealing barley from a barn across the river at Litlington. He served his sentence and returned to be employed by the Rector of Herstmonceux as manservant and later footman.

The house was, and may still be, a warren ideally suited for a smuggler. There were 21 rooms, 47 doors and 6 staircases as well as cellars and a hiding space in the roof. After standing for several centuries it was severely damaged when in July 2004 a car was driven into it in the early hours, was reversed out and disappeared into the night. The Inn opened again within days but considerable restoration works were needed that were finally completed in 2005.

It is a long, slow climb out of Alfriston but it does get better as you ascend: much better with long, sweeping views to the north over the Weald and south to the sea.

After about two kilometres it is possible to look down from the front edge of the escarpment on the long bulk of the great barn at Alciston. one of the ancient villages sitting at the foot of the Downs. At 170 feet (59 metres) the barn is one of the longest in England and probably the largest in Sussex. Like many another great barn it is called a tithe barn but probably was not. The manor belonged to the church through Battle Abbey and its primary purpose would have been to store the whole produce of an estate that belonged to the church not just to collect the tenth of the produce of others that was due to the church.

And we have only travelled a short distance before reaching a problem with another of those Sussex names. Alciston is, of course, pronounced Ahlston.

Further ahead on the way up to Firle Beacon there is the car park at Bopeep. Here hang gliders can often be seen casting themselves off into thin air from the top of the escarpment. Just below there is the disused Bopeep Chalk Pit, Bopeep Farm is halfway down and Bopeep Bostal runs up from the village down below.

The village also has another of those difficult names. It is spelt Selmeston but should be pronounced Simpson. It is not in honour of a transatlantic cartoon family of varied hues that it predates by many years. The authority for the pronunciation is the Rev William Parish who was vicar there for over 40 years until his death in 1904. Amongst his many accomplishments was the publication in 1875 of his **Dictionary of the Sussex Dialect**. He mentions the pronunciation of the name of the village in his introduction to the dictionary. We also learn from the dictionary that the word 'bostal' means, "*A pathway up a hill, generally a very steep one, and on the northern escarpment of the Downs*".

One of the Rev Parish's friends was Lewis Carrol and there was a local rumour, almost certainly unfounded, that **Alice in Wonderland** was written in the vicarage down below. But the "*queer stuffed bird which the vicar's brother sent from South America*" may have been the origin of the Jabberwock which, "*with eyes of flame*",

> "*Came whiffling through the tulgey wood,*
> *And burbled as it came.*"

We probably have a stereotype image of Little Bopeep from childhood days: calf length crinoline dress, with lacey unmentionables peeking below, sun bonnet, crook swathed with ribbons and lambs gambolling about a well turned ankle. Reality is somewhat different. Although the Downs here are sheep country, bopeep has nothing to do with sheep. It's suggested that it is "*a sardonic reference to a turnpike keeper peeping through his small window*" through which he collected the tolls but it is apparently a name that is not uncommon in smuggling country. So who was watching whom: smugglers looking out for Revenue Officers or vice-versa, especially as Selmeston was a depot where incoming goods were stored for onwards distribution.

Bopeep is also a crossing of the ways: north/south, east/west. The roads that can be seen, and they are roads whatever they may look like now, were used by the Romans and had been used by others for thousands of years before that. The north/south route was a well trodden smugglers' route up from Seaford down to the depot at Selmeston below.

It might be said that up on the South Downs Way we are out in the sticks. Two or three thousand years ago the sticks were more likely to have been in the Weald down below: heavy woodland and even heavier clay soil. In some places along the downs you can get an impression of what it must have been like, seemingly unending woodland. It was not wholly impenetrable. There are traces down there of Mesolithic man (Middle Stone Age c12000 to 4000 BC) and of local clearances but why go down there when there was lighter, more easily worked soil on the Downs and there was no pressure for land from an increasing population.

Up on the Downs we are the latest of a long line stretching back into prehistory and we are following in their footsteps. People travelled along the ancient ways along the Downs. They lived on the Downs in villages and camps on the which there are some traces. They occupied hill forts of which there are more than just traces. They died up there and the barrows, the tumuli, scattered across the map, some of which are passed on this section, are the most plentiful remains of those who lived and died there.

There are long barrows and round barrows and the long barrows have been here longer and that is an easy way to remember that they came first. They are both believed to have been the final coverings of sacred areas where the dead were laid and ritual carried out rather than just being tombs for one burial and the siting of barrows had much do with territoriality and control of the landscape

The long barrows come from the Neolithic (New Stone Age c4000-2000 BC) when farming and a more settled way of life had developed. They are between 30 and 90 metres long and higher and wider at one end, usually the east, where the burials took place. They were used over a period of years for a number of interments and held an average of 6 bodies. It must be admitted that those on the Marlborough Downs south of Avebury are far more impressive than those that remain on the South Downs.

The round barrows come mainly from the Bronze Age (c2000-700 BC) although they continued on into Roman times and beyond into Saxon when they were finally succeeded by cemeteries which were normal by about 700 AD. There does not seem to be any common theme: practices and ritual varied. There were both single and multiple burials. Bodies were buried as well as the ashes of those who had been cremated. An expert can distinguish 12 different types. Bowl barrows, with or without a ditch immediately surrounding the mound, are the most common. Bell barrows are those where ditch lies further away from the mound with a flat area between ditch and mound.

Most barrows have a depression at the top. This usually indicates inexpert excavation, mainly Victorian, often to get the non existent treasure that was believed to be inside.

Some barrows have names from when the original purpose had been long forgotten and, sometimes, the supernatural was believed to be the cause. The Devil's Jumps lie by the Way some way ahead. He was also very busy elsewhere a bit further along.

At 217 metres (712 feet) Firle Beacon is the highest point on this block of the downs and probably the joint highest point on the path of the South Downs Way. Butser Hill ahead in Hampshire is the highest hill of the South Downs but the path does not reach as far as the top of that. Round barrows are passed on the way up to Firle Beacon and if you wonder why, when you get there, the Trig Point does not appear to be at the highest point, the mound beside it is what remains of a long barrow.

Northwards from Firle Beacon the roof of the new Opera House at Glyndebourne can be seen rising above the trees. Sir John Christie founded his world renowned private opera house in 1934. It has been almost as well known as part of the social scene as for the excellence of its productions. Audiences in evening dress travelled by train from London with their picnic baskets for alfresco meals and champagne by the lake. The excellence still prevails enhanced by the new 1,150-seat house that was opened in 1994.

To the south of Glyndebourne closer into the Downs the cupola above the stables of Glynde Place can be seen in the middle of the village of Glynde. John Ellman, usually known as John Ellman of Glynde, (1753-1832) had his farm at Glynde from 1780 to 1829. And a patriarchal figure he was.

He lodged his unmarried labourers in his own home and when they married gave them enough land for a pig, a cow and a garden. He built a school for the children of Glynde and protected the inhabitants from a public house in the village. It was not that he was an abstainer. He believed that beer was the true drink of the farm labourer but that they should brew it at home rather than buying it across a bar.

He also made a considerable contribution to farming especially in improving the Southdown breed of sheep by selection from within the breed. The Southdown became the foundation of many a flock at home and abroad,

even reaching the estates of the Tsar of Russia as well as South Africa, Australia and especially New Zealand. His rams commanded high sale prices and stud fees and his sheep won many a prize in shows. The Southdown is now an endangered breed but interest in them appears to be increasing.

Now rarely seen on the Downs

About 400 metres beyond Firle Beacon and its long barrow you move at least 2,000 years forward to the Romans. The received wisdom appears to be that Roman roads went straight ahead in one continuous line, deviating neither right nor left, come what may. That is not wholly true; Roman engineers were more practical than that and avoided putting themselves in impossible situations. Their roads do usually run dead straight for mile after mile but the Romans were not willing to plunge straight off the escarpment like the hang gliders but without wings. So it is above the village of West Firle. The terrace way, known as the Rabbit Walk, that takes you down to the village, is Roman engineering and we are back again to that continuity with the past.

Firle Place, hidden by the trees, has belonged to the Gage family since the 15th century. Although privately owned it is opened to the public at certain times of the year and achieves a 4 star rating in Simon Jenkins' ***England's Thousand Best Houses***. There is also a public footpath passing through the park.

All the great houses beneath the Downs have more than one story of those who lived there or what happened there. So it is with Firle Place. A personal favourite is of Lady Penelope who no storyteller could conceive as being anything other than beautiful. At the age of 17 she had three suitors, one of whom was Sir John Gage of Firle. Whether she could not make up her mind, whether it was that she loved them all, whether it was to stop them quarrelling over her, but she promised them that she would marry each in turn; and so she did. First, Sir John Trenchard but he did not last very long. Then, at a discreet interval, Sir John Gage. Nine children later, he died in 1653 – one almost wonders why it was not her rather than him – and she married Sir William Hervey, her third suitor. He outlived her.

The tower on the hill below is not a folly. It had a very practical purpose. It was built by the Gages so that their gamekeepers could keep a look out for poachers. Close to you can see that it has a chimney and that the windows are glazed.

Later, the hill across the valley guarding the way into Lewes is The Caburn. For the purists, it is said that this is pronounced CAWBURN. It is also said that the name comes from the Celtic *Caer bryn*, meaning fort on the hill. If so it is one of the few surviving names directly reminding us of the Celts who once occupied most of Britain. They built the Iron Age Forts that dominated so many tops, including Caburn itself. Apparently the name does not appear to have been recorded until the 18th century but that does not mean to say that it was not in local usage for centuries before that.

Caburn could also have been impressed into service in later years. In the late 18th century, amidst fears of a French invasion, plans were drawn up for Caburn, Cissbury and Hollingbury, all ancient hillforts, to be held as advance defence posts together with other castles, churches and windmills.

Most of the old names on the Downs and in Sussex are now from the Saxons: Sussex was the kingdom of the South Saxons. Saxon rule displaced the Celtic Romano British over a period of many years. The perceived wisdom has been that was by wiping them out, possibly delayed by King Arthur, or pushing them further west into Wales and Cornwall. It was probably more by assimilation. The latest research indicates that the Saxons do not appear to be the unwelcome or overwhelming force that they were later made to appear. Archaeology reveals a continuity of farming methods and occupation of sites with no evidence of violent disruption; and, although the far reaching power of the Roman Empire was declining, there was nevertheless an increasing burden of taxation from the central authority in Rome for a diminishing return; never a popular measure especially when a better alternative may have been provided nearer to home by the Saxons.

So it is that many of the places that we pass through or close to on the Way have component parts from Old English spoken by the Saxons. The 'ton' in Alfriston meaning the farmstead of Ælfric, not Alfred: the 'ing' of Ditchling or Poynings meaning 'the people of' (Dicel and Puna respectively: Puna meaning the Hammer): the 'combe' of Pyecombe and Saddlescombe meaning 'valley'. It is a slightly false construction to claim that Billingshurst is the hurst or wooded hill of the people of Bill – a letter out: it was Billa (meaning 'the Dagger') whose people may have been those who also settled at Billingsgate. Is it merely coincidence that Stane Street, the old Roman road between Chichester and London that will be encountered further along the Way, passes through Billingshurst to end at London Bridge with Billingsgate Market just beyond the bridge?

The word 'Downs' itself also comes from the Saxons but why is it Downs when they are so obviously up? It is actually the other way round. Why do we descend by going down when, originally, 'down' meant up. The word 'down' comes from an Old English word dun which means hill. Down, in the sense of going downwards is a corruption of the Old English adun – from or off the hill – so, downhill. But the word dun is another example of that assimilation and continuity being borrowed by the Saxons from the British and meaning an uninhabited hill.

There may be a geological explanation why Caburn lies apart from the main range of the Downs but as any reasonable person knows it was where one of the clods of earth fell when the Devil was excavating Devil's Dyke. There are also legends of treasure buried up there. There are said to be, in separate caches, a silver coffin and a knight in golden armour. It is possible that these are protected by the Devil like other Sussex treasure, and, when you dig in the right place, He just moves the treasure away.

The Way descends Itford Hill into the valley of the Sussex Ouse to cross the river at Southease bridge where it meets the Sussex Ouse Valley Way for a short while. The Sussex Ouse Valley Way was opened in 2005. It was created by Per-Rambulations with the support and encouragement of the County Councils of East and West Sussex and the Sussex Downs Conservation Board (now the South Downs Joint Committee). 42 miles long, the Sussex Ouse Valley Way traces the valley of the Sussex Ouse and its river from source to sea through the rich diversity of the Sussex countryside.

Long gone are the days when the Ouse formed the basis of a navigational system from the sea at Newhaven as far inland to the Ouse Valley Viaduct near Balcombe. The viaduct was one of the engineering marvels of the Victorian Age and still in constant use today over 150 years later to carry a main railway line. Most of the 11 million bricks used to build the viaduct were carried upstream on barges through here, some of them from the brickworks that were a mile or so downstream at Piddinghoe.

The bridge at Southease is a swing bridge to allow the traffic through. It cannot now be opened but you can see a curve in the planking at the western end of the bridge where it opened and the winding mechanism can still be seen underneath the bridge.

The Lower Navigation between Lewes and Newhaven carried regular commercial traffic until 1927. There was still some commercial use of the lower reaches until the 1950s. It is still used by pleasure craft.

Commercial operations on the Upper Navigation above Lewes stopped in 1868. It was in a ruinous condition by the end of the 19th century. SORT, the Sussex Ouse Restoration Trust, has, however, ambitious plans to restore the locks and make the Upper Ouse navigable again. These include proposals that could alleviate flooding at Lewes.

From Southease Bridge Lewes Castle can be seen upstream. The castle is a reminder of the Normans who completed the last successful foreign invasion of England after the Celts, the Romans and, in this part of the world, the Saxons, if invasion is the right word for the Romans and the Saxons. This is not from a misplaced desire for political correctness. 'Invasion' implies military intervention and it is highly likely that the Romans and the Saxons came to the south east more by encouragement than force.

The strategic importance of the castle can be appreciated from the bridge. It dominates the landscape far more than from almost any other viewpoint and it commanded the Rape of Lewes.

The rapes as a territorial division are unique to Sussex. There are six of them. They were probably created by the Normans to control the natural points of invasion and they were originally held by William's most trusted followers. They are Hastings, Pevensey, Lewes, Bramber, Arundel and Chichester. Essentially they are six parallel strips of land running northwards from the south coast. They had a number of things in common; a port, or what was once a port, a river, a road to London, and a strong castle to control the lot. They were possibly to control the points of invasion but could equally have been to secure means of escape if invasion and colonisation failed.

Rape most probably comes from an old Norse word for rope. It is still used in that sense in Bosham, a Sussex haven for yachtsmen, where the *Raptackle*, an ancient wooden building is still used for storing ropes and tackle. And why not use a rope for measuring? We have, or pre-metric, used to have, rods, poles and chains. There is also the story that Richard Fitzgilbert, one of William's supporters, measured the boundaries of his castle at Brione with a rope so that he could check to see that he was getting as much as he was giving up. He was not dissatisfied. He got nearly 200 English manors spread across 8 counties.

The South Downs Way passes the church at Southease with its round tower. There are only three churches in Sussex with round towers and they are all in the Ouse Valley. The other two are at Piddinghoe downstream and in Lewes itself. Nobody knows why these should have round towers. One suggestion has been that they were designed as a series of beacon towers. The most likely explanation appears to be that flint, the local building material, comes in small pieces and it is not easy to build it in square shapes without stone quoins or corners.

As an indication of how the landscape and the course of the river here have changed over the centuries, Southease was once a fishing village and was assessed in 1089 AD for 38,500 herrings and £4 for porpoises annually.

Virginia Woolf is one of those figures in English Literature about whom opinions are sharply divided. One of her claims to fame is that she introduced what is called *"the stream of consciousness"* method into novel writing. She, if not her novels, is likely to become better known from the film **The Hours** (2003), starring Nicole Kidman complete with prosthetic nose in an episode featuring the novelist.

Virginia and her husband, Leonard Woolf, lived the last years of her life at Monks House at Rodmell less than a mile away to the north west of Southease Bridge. In 1941 she committed suicide by drowning herself in the Ouse. Her home at Rodmell now belongs to the National Trust and is open to the public at certain times of the year. The village can be reached by an easy diversion from what is now the Way along a section that was formerly on the route of the South Downs Way.

A right turn along the road above Southease for just over half a mile (700 metres) will lead straight to the conveniently placed Abergavenny Arms at Rodmell. Care should be taken as the road is fast and busy but there is a verge that should be used. The route then takes a left turn opposite the Abergavenny Arms up Mill Hill to rejoin the what has become the 'official' Way after 800 metres. The blacksmith's forge stands on the right corner at the start of Mill Hill.

There is a photograph in Miles Jebb's **A guide to the South Downs Way** (1984) showing Frank Dean the blacksmith, or more properly the farrier, standing at the door of the forge with Achnacarry, one of his 'customers' and Miles Jebb's companion along the South Downs Way. In 1952 Frank Dean had succeeded his father at the forge, his father having taken over the forge in

1910. Frank Dean was still working at the forge in 2004 when, sadly, in July, after completing a full day's work, he died at the age of 87. He, in turn, is succeeded by his son and grandson. You may not be lucky enough to see the forge working. Nowadays blacksmiths (or farriers) visit the horses instead of the other way around.

During the course of this section there is a crossing from east to west, stepping over the imaginary line of the Greenwich Meridian: 0 degrees of longitude. You may be forgiven for missing it. There is no border post or line scratched in the surface of the track. There is no discernible change in the landscape. Local customs and language stay the same.

It is not possible to point it accurately in words without some recognisable feature on the ground, but, after crossing the road above Southease, there is a short descent into a valley. The Way follows the valley for about a kilometre before climbing the shoulder of Mill Hill where it is crossed by a footpath close to some houses. The meridian crosses the Way about 500 metres further on, about 75 metres short of being crossed by another footpath – and that's the best that can be done.

Coming towards the end of this section the Way travels along a track running between Brighton and Lewes known as Jugg's Road. 'Juggs' was a nickname for the Brighton fishermen, possibly from earthenware, although some say leather, jugs used to carry their fish fresh to market.

Other Sussex fishermen had their nicknames too. For some unknown reason, those from Worthing were 'pork-bolters' or 'pork-boilers' and those from Eastbourne were 'willock-eaters', a willock being a guillemot and somewhat unsavoury in taste. The Hastings fishermen are apparently insulted by being called 'Chop-Backs' a reference to a fight in 1768 when a gang of pirates based in Hastings boarded a Dutch ship, killing the captain in the process by chopping through his spine with an axe.

The last word on fishing for now, is from that great fisherman, Izaak Walton, who we will also meet again on the Way. In his book, **The Compleat Angler**, he wrote, "*Just so doth Sussex boast of four sorts of fish, namely, a Arundel Mullet, a Chichester Lobster, a Shelsey (sic) Cockle, and an Amerly (sic) Trout*". It is a long time since there were trout at Amberley apart from any that may be served in the restaurant at Amberley Castle.

A27 to Devil's Dyke

"But we who've stood on Ditchling,
And watch'd the red sun set
Behind the Hills at Fulking –
We shall not soon forget,
Mount Harry, grey and quiet,
Crown'd Cissbury tinged with fire,
Or royal, happy Ditchling,
The Haven of desire"

Alfred Bathurst Norman
From ***Ditchling Beacon***

Some years ago when it was noticed that traffic on the A27 was becoming thicker and faster and that walkers of a certain age were less fleet of foot than they had been, the South Downs Way was diverted. Crossing the A27 via the old route is, at best, a spectator sport, somewhat like horizontal bunjee jumping without the rubber band. The official route now crosses the A27 by a bridge, returning part way eastwards before turning northwards up on to the Downs. It is safe and does not give walk leaders any unnecessary palpitations when it is used by the walkers (and also stops walk leaders from offering odds on the success rate).

Towards the top of the Downs, one turns left (west) to follow the ridge with the sweeping views over the Weald leaving behind three hills that continue the ridge eastwards.

The nearest is Blackcap at 206 metres (676 feet). It got its name from the dark clump of pines on its summit. An earlier clump became a casualty of war from the military training that took place across the Downs during World War II. It was replanted in 1953 to mark the coronation of Queen Elizabeth II. Ben Darby in ***The South Downs*** (1976) was not wholly optimistic about it regaining "*its old look of dark drama*" but it now seems to have regained its former brooding presence.

Beyond Blackcap is Mount Harry, a bit lower at 194 metres (636 feet) and then Offham (pronounced OAFHAM) Hill. That is possibly the most important ground on the Downs. It was there that the Battle of Lewes started on 4th May 1264. Baronial forces under Simon de Montfort defeated King Henry III and for a short time a form of parliamentary government was established until Simon's death at the Battle of Evesham a year later.

Simon Scharma (**A History of Britain**) says that the date 1264 is more momentous for the development of English democracy than the sealing of Magna Carta by King John (Henry III's father) nearly 50 years before in 1215. In both cases the barons opposing the Crown might be a little surprised that they are credited with creating foundation stones of human liberty and parliamentary democracy as we know them, but undoubtedly the first stirrings were there.

A king did not lose his throne hereabouts and the subjects are no longer in danger of losing their shirts on a misplaced faith on a 'certainty' or the predictive power of a pin. Above Lewes on the Downs and not far from the battlefield is the site of what was once Lewes racecourse. The grandstand and some of the railings are still there and ground is still used for training gallops but the racing, of which the records date back to 1727, ended on 14 September 1964. The Horserace Betting Levy Board had decided to subsidise it no longer. The course was difficult of public access, exposed to the weather, the prize money was meagre and the allocated meetings were mostly on a Monday: rather like doing the South Downs Way apart from being restricted to Mondays.

The racecourse was closed during World War II but many of the jockeys and stable lads who were over the age of conscription joined the Lewes Mounted Home Guard to patrol the Downs against incursions by enemy troops. If they had been available they could also have been useful before that war when in the 1920s and 1930s Lewes racecourse was infected by the razor gangs that operated protection rackets, extracting 'insurance premiums' from bookmakers. There are records of gang attacks and razor slashings. Lewes was not alone in suffering in that way. Similar troubles in the same period were not far away at the racecourse at Brighton. These were immortalised by Graham Greene in his novel **Brighton Rock** (1938), later filmed in 1947 with a young Richard Attenborough in the lead.

Paul Millmore in his **South Downs Way** (Revised edition 2004) mentions snails in this section but does not go into further detail. The rather handsome, large, pinkish snail that can seen along the Way from time to time is the Edible or Roman snail. Edible it is: Roman it is not. It is a native and was here long before the Romans came. It inhabits the chalk lands of south east England. It is protected in some countries as an endangered species for it has a more international identity. It is the variety that is billed on menus as Escargots although impersonators sometimes creep in to take its place.

Stretches of concrete road running up to and across the Downs have and will be encountered. Most, and probably all, are relics of World War II. At first the impetus was to reclaim land to grow cereal crops but in 1942, 22,000 acres of downland between Eastbourne and Littlehampton were requisitioned for military training. This included provision for a range for armoured fighting vehicles at Seaford Head and its surrounding countryside. The people living in the high farms were evacuated, the requisitioned land was closed to civilians and the roads were laid.

Many of those high farms and other buildings were used for target practice. There is that sad photograph showing a forlorn Belle Tout lighthouse battered and shell pierced. The lighthouse came back but other damaged buildings never returned.

The high spot of the day is Ditchling Beacon at 248 metres (814 feet) and on a hot day the ice cream van that is usually there can be a truly welcoming sight. It is not known but thought highly unlikely that the riders in the Tour de France formed an orderly queue there when the race came up the hill some years ago when the Tour routed through part of southern England, but neither riders nor motorists were able to get up the bostal in 2003 when it was closed by snow.

A mile beyond Ditchling Beacon there is another crossing at Keymer Post: from East Sussex to West Sussex with the whole of West Sussex now to cross before passing into Hampshire near Buriton (*Berryton*). There is nothing on the post to show that it marks the border. One arm points back to Eastbourne: one points forward to the goal at Winchester: Brighton is shown to the south and Keymer to the north. There is a plaque let into the foot of the Post on which the inscription reads:

"Peter and Philippa
Loved life and each other
Together now and forever
Both aged 21 years
23rd September 1994"

Peter and Philippa were an engaged couple who loved walking. They were killed a tragic jet ski accident in Turkey.

The Way passes close to the Clayton windmills. They can be reached by another short diversion.

The smaller whited painted 'Jill' is a post mill. She was built in 1821 at Brighton and was brought to Clayton from Dyke Road by wagon around 1850. She is in working order and is sometimes open to the public. The taller 'Jack' is a tower mill built in 1876 and now a private residence.

A post mill is one where the mill is mounted on a mighty central pillar or post and the whole of the main structure turns to bring the sails, or sweeps as they are known in Sussex, into the wind. With a tower mill, the main structure is static; only the top cap bearing the sweeps turns.

Jack is a tower mill and not a smock mill as some of the books say. A smock mill works on the same principle as a tower mill with only the top cap turning but is timber framed and clad in wood. For that reason it is polygonal and not round like a tower mill.

Jack has another claim to fame. He was the eponymous hero of the 1974 film **The Black Windmill** in which he co-starred with Michael Caine. The critics were not overly impressed by the film. Jack's role is not mentioned but presumably it was somewhat static. The forces of evil, however, were overcome.

Wolstonbury Hill stands in advance of the main rank of the Downs. It gives outstanding views and is crowned by what has been called a fort. It was created in the late Bronze Age and is unusual in that the ditch is inside the rampart instead of outside. This led some writers to ponder on the mystery of why that should be, almost implying that the builders must have had the blueprints upside down. A verderer, one who is responsible for a deer forest, would not have had the same difficulty. That was the way forest boundaries were constructed: ditch inside and rampart out to keep animals in and not people out. The earthwork was not a fort as it had been called but an enclosure with a far more peaceful purpose.

Also at the top there are depressions left by flint diggings but these are from the 19th century, probably for building materials, not from any part of the Stone Age.

The big house to the left (west) at the foot of Wolstonbury Hill is Danny. It is Elizabethan and was built for the Dacre family somewhere between 1582 and 1595. It was sold to Peter Courthorpe in 1652. His only daughter married Henry Campion and Danny stayed in the ownership of the Campion family until 1980 when James Campion, the then owner, who worked with the poor in India, sold it. A medical centre in Madras was built from the sale proceeds. Danny was converted into luxury retirement apartments and that was still the use in 2004.

Do buildings like people have their 15 minutes of fame? It was down there in 1918 that members of the Imperial War Cabinet, including Lloyd George and Winston Churchill, met to work out the terms of the Armistice to end fighting in the First World War. It is said that Lloyd George used to take papers up Wolstonbury Hill when he wanted to work in peace and quiet.

The lovers of tea and cakes are no longer catered for at Pyecombe at the tea shop in the Old Forge opposite the church with its tower capped by the pyramid roof known as a Sussex Cap. It was there at the forge, deep in sheep country, that Pyecombe Crooks, or hooks, were made with their distinctive long guides and small heads. An example of a shepherd's hook, larger than life-size, is fixed to the gate into the churchyard.

The expression 'by hook or by crook', meaning to get or do something by any means possible, once meant the opposite and does not come wholly from shepherds' hooks or crooks. In Medieval times the poor were allowed to gather dead wood from forests for firewood provided that the only implements used were a hook (a blunt billhook) or a shepherds crook to extend their reach to pull dead wood down. Other means were forbidden: nothing sharp: no saws, axes or the like. One was allowed to gather only what could be had by these limited methods: not get anything that was going in any way fair or foul.

The gate to the churchyard is also distinctive. It is a Tapsell gate; one that

pivots in the middle instead of being hinged at one end. Nobody knows why they are called Tapsell gates but Tapsell is a Sussex name and, as these gates are peculiar to Sussex, it has been suggested that a local family were responsible for them. In addition to keeping livestock out, they make it easier for a laden coffin to be carried in.

Although crops have been grown on the top of the Downs for thousands of years to a greater or lesser extent depending upon economic conditions and the need to grow food, particularly in time of war, agriculture on the Downs is perceived as being almost synonymous with sheep. But sheep were part of an integrated system that operated for centuries. On the Downs their original principal purpose was not the production of meat or wool but as living muck spreaders. During the day they would roam the hills in their thousands under the care of their shepherds, during the night they would be folded on the arable fields of their home farm to enrich the soil in the traditional and natural way.

It was, of course, necessary to keep a check on the sheep by counting them. It is said that counting sheep is soporific. That may be so but, if it does not work for you, it may be that the right method of counting is not being used.

On the Downs the sheep were driven through a pair of hurdles or a gate and the shepherd would count pairs of sheep as they passed through using his own numbers. These varied from place to place and from shepherd to shepherd but a representative sample is:

1	One-erum	6	Sath-erum
2	Two-erum	7	Wineberry
3	Cock-erum	8	Wagtail
4	Shu-erum	9	Tarry Diddle
5	Sith-erum	10	Den.

As the sheep were counted in pairs 'den' marked twenty, otherwise a score, and a notch was cut in a tally stick. Obviously the shepherd was keeping a tally but was this also keeping the score? And Hambledon, the 'Cradle of Cricket' is on the South Downs.

It is not inappropriate that Saddlescombe Farm that stands guard at the threshold of the great coombe excavated by the Devil should once have been a preceptory of Knights Templar, the order of warrior monks that was founded to protect pilgrims in the Holy Land. They were 'The Poor Fellow-Soldiers of Jesus Christ and the Temple of Solomon'. Individual knights were governed by vows of poverty but the Order grew rich and powerful. The Templars not only created the first uniformed standing army in the west since the days of Roman rule there but also laid the foundations of modern international banking. They were advisors to popes and kings. Much of their property, mainly land, came by way of gift from those who must have been motivated, at least in part, by the hope that it would assist the passage to Heaven. The Manor of Saddlescombe and other property was granted to the Order in 1228 by Geoffrey de Say. It is highly unlikely that it would ever have echoed to the clash of arms or the stamp of the war-horse. As a preceptory it was part of the investment portfolio producing income to keep the monks on the battlefield.

In spite of the Templar industry that has boomed of late, it is not inconceivable that the suppression of the Order by the Catholic Church starting from 1307 arose from the highly coloured and probably almost wholly unfounded charges that were levelled against the Order by the French King, Philip IV; "almost" as some of the alleged practices, if true, may have been to condition those who might be taken prisoner against torture. Philip was in pressing need of funds and, no doubt, was casting somewhat envious eyes towards the supposed riches of the Order. He had undertaken, and was to undertake, similar manoeuvres against others both before and afterwards. There is some irony that the Templars' resources, or, according to some, those that were found, were transferred to the Knights Hospitaller rather than falling into the royal coffers either of France or of those monarchies that followed its example: some did not.

No treasure was found at Saddlescombe. In her delightful book **A South Downs Farm in the 1860s** Maude Robinson lists the possessions at Saddlescombe at the time of the transfer to the Hospitallers including the household contents of "*three trestle tables, one chair, two brass pots, two dishes, one towel and one cup*".

There were 900 acres at Saddlesombe in the 1860s. On the basis of one sheep per acre, there were three separate flocks of sheep of 300 each plus all the other usual farming activities, and twelve oxen for ploughing, the same number that the Templars had over 500 years before. It was what many would think was a hard, restricted life but it comes through from the book as rich and rewarding no matter how lacking it may seem in alleged modern advantages. And who is to say that the power to use one's imagination and apply one's knowledge is not more liberating than an increasingly regulated modern existence.

But we must not forget the Donkey Wheel that Maude Robinson calls the 'Well-Wheel' for it was not always powered by a donkey to bring up water from the well. It depended on what was available: donkey, horse or man. There were the donkeys: old, white, bad tempered Smoker, whose passing was not mourned, and grey Issachar that the three youngest children used to ride at once; and there was the pony Com, short for Commodore Nut. Of men working the wheel she leaves no record

save that it was tedious work and, maybe, there were other tasks elsewhere on the farm that they found had priority when water had to be drawn.

There cannot have been many idle hands around the farms of Sussex for idle hands make the Devil's work and the Devil rarely comes to Sussex. It may well be that is because the good cooks of Sussex can make almost anything into a pudding and that is what the Devil most fears may happen to him. But sometimes circumstances force him to come.

Christianity came later to Sussex than to many other parts of England but, when it did come, it was embraced with enthusiasm. Churches sprang up the length and breadth of the Weald: far more than the Devil could tolerate.

He hit on the idea of digging a ditch through the Downs so that the sea would flood in and drown the churches. One night he set to work shovelling like mad. Shovelfuls hurtled everywhere. As we know one became Caburn; others were Chanctonbury and Cissbury and Rackham Hills. The trench now known as Devil's Dyke advanced rapidly towards the sea.

Some would have us believe that it was a man that saved the day: one of the local saints: Cuthman or Dunstan. But that is mere chauvinistic propaganda.

The truth lies with a little old lady. Disturbed by the sound of frantic digging, she lit her candle and made her way to the window. The Devil caught sight of the glimmer of light out of the corner of his eye. He had been engrossed in his task and believing that time had passed more quickly than it had, thought that it was the first rays of the morning sun. As if to confirm it, a cock crowed. In these days people shared their homes with their livestock and in jigging about to get a better view, the old lady had knocked her cockerel off his perch. He protested loudly.

But it was enough for the Devil. As far as he was concerned day was dawning and the pudding bowl was waiting. Off he flew, trench unfinished and the Weald saved. And, it is said, as he flew over the Channel a great clod of earth and chalk fell from some part of his anatomy to become Isle of Wight.

If you are using Devil's Dyke as the end of a stage, have a while before you leave, and the day is clear, pause at the toposcope overlooking the escarpment to see where you have come from and where you are going. The view over the Way to the east is not extensive. Beyond Newtimber Hill the white cap and sails of Jack, the tower mill at Clayton, can be seen peeping over the trees but the rising ground towards Ditchling Beacon cuts off any further view. There can, however, be long, wide views northwards over the Weald that take in Blackdown, the highest point in Sussex, and, over the Downs to the west, there may be sights of Butser Hill in Hampshire, 33 miles away, the highest point on the South Downs, and to Crown Tegleaze the highest point on the Sussex Downs.

Devil's Dyke to Washington

"Say what you will, – there is not in the world
A nobler sight than from this upper down,
No rugged landscape here, no beauty hurled
From its Creator's hand as with a frown;
But a green plain on which green hills look down
Trim as a garden plot."

Wilfred Scawen Blunt
(1840-1922)
From ***Chanclebury Ring***

If one is using Devil's Dyke as a staging point and leaving from or going to the car park in front of the Dyke Hotel, the temptation is to cut a corner and use the footpath that passes closer to the edge of the escarpment than the route of the South Downs Way. The purist will, no doubt, if going westward, walk back along the road from the car park to rejoin the Way or, if going eastwards, stay on the Way until reaching the road. That purist will pass on the other side and gain a better impression of the bank built to create the Iron Age fort on top of Dyke Hill that now carries a trig point.

'Fort' may give a misleading impression of the larger enclosures that are called 'forts'. In spite of the defences, both man made and natural, they would have needed considerable manpower to defend successfully: possibly more than would have been available at the time. A home for some they may also have been places of tribal gathering and trading, to mark boundaries or, high on a hill top, when the ditches were at their full depth and the banks to their full height topped by wooden ramparts, to impress the neighbours. The enclosure on Devil's Dyke is 15 hectares (37 acres) in extent and best appreciated by walking its boundaries or from aerial photographs.

When written records for Britain started with the Romans, some were called *oppida*, cities, and that may more truly express the purpose of the bigger ones. That too may explain the verse in Kiplings' ***Puck's Song***:

"See you our pastures wide and lone,
Where the red oxen browse?
O there was a City thronged and known
Ere London boasted a house."

But a burning topic of conversation to cover the first (or last) mile or so will no doubt be, *"What is the Dyke?"* It is a bit like, *"Why are the Downs up?"* Is it the coombe or valley that was excavated by the Devil or He, with a capital H, as they sometimes say in Sussex to avoid using His, again with a capital H, name? Or is it that built up bank of earth of the Iron Age enclosure on the top?

Ordinary dictionaries are not much help. They take the easy way but unhelpful way out – their definitions give both meanings, but a later editor of the Rev Parish's **Dictionary of the Sussex Dialect** is emphatic that it means, *"A built up bank or earth wall"*. Take your pick but custom now dictates that Devil's Dyke is the great ditch and not what may have come out of a ditch.

The road between Dyke Hill and Brighton was described as being in the 1870s, *"one of the dustiest in England, and … overrun with holiday-makers in various stages of drunkenness – noisy, ill-looking, offensive"* – and any obvious easy comments about those walking the South Downs Way are to be avoided.

Those holiday-makers, and those who were to come after them, were on their way to a popular place of entertainment. Not only were there spectacular views and the opportunity for more refreshment, but there were a variety of other attractions that varied over the years and plans for others that, mercifully, did not materialise.

From 1887 until 1939, those holiday makers could save themselves from the dust by catching a steam train up from Brighton. It is still possible to walk the route of that railway from Hangleton. On the way it passes the site of the Golf Club halt that was opened in 1891. There, alas, was only a platform and name board; lighting and shelter were lacking. Passengers could wait in the club house 50 yards away, and, in 1895, the railway company installed a bell in the club house that gave sufficient warning to enable drinks to be finished and the platform reached before the train arrived. Was it of this course that E V Lucas, the doyen of modern Sussex travel writers, wrote in 1904, *"Ladies also play golf where, when I first knew it, one could walk unharmed"*.

At the top one could enjoy more railway treats.

There was the Dyke Steep-Grade Railway on the north facing escarpment. From personal experience this would have been infinitely preferable to coming up the escarpment on foot and at a fare of 2 old pence (somewhat less than 1p) well worth the price. It was a funicular railway that was opened in 1897 and climbed down to Poynings below on a cable. It did not have a long life. The proprietor of the attractions on Dyke Hill did not like his customers using his railway to sample the rival delights of the tea rooms and public houses in Poynings. It seems to have ceased operations in 1908 although there may have been some limited use after that. It is still possible to trace foundations of the engine house and the upper end platform close to the pub.

Then, from 1896, for an extra sixpence (2½p but do not forget inflation) one could sweep 1,100 feet across the chasm of the Dyke itself on a cableway. A maximum height of 230 feet above the ground was reached in a cage suitable for four passengers, or six sheep: not that one supposes that sheep often availed themselves of the opportunity to make use of the facility. This too was not wholly successful and closed in 1909. Again it is still possible to trace some evidence on the ground of this ride from concrete bases for the masts that supported the cables.

On solid land there was an amusement park with rides and swings and side shows and tearooms and at one time, in more recent years, a zoo. Other attractions were planned. Just after World War II these included a full-scale windmill and a replica Egyptian temple set into the wall of the Dyke that fortunately did not come to pass. Perhaps most relief might be felt at the failure of the plan in the 1920s and 1930s to build a national motor racing circuit close to the Devil's Dyke. That would have produced a 4½ mile track enclosing 450 acres and capable of accommodating 50,000 spectators.

Most of the amusements took place on a comparatively small area within the little excavated fort or enclosure that occupies the top of the hill. It is a promontory fort created by building that large bank across the neck of land separating Dyke Hill from the remainder of the Downs and relying mainly on the natural defences of the Dyke itself and the escarpment for the remainder of the perimeter.

About one and a half kilometres (1 mile) further on from the road crossing at Devil's Dyke one can see a patch of vegetation with terracing some 400 metres to the south of the Way. Any disturbance in the smooth contours of the Downs is usually a sign of interference by man and this marks the site of the medieval village of Perching. Emptied neither by plague nor raves at Devil's Dyke that were to lay in the future Perching appears to have been a casualty of economics and changing agricultural practices. In 1327 there were fourteen taxable residents but, taking families into account, the actual population would have been higher. Five years later the taxpayers had been reduced to 11 but the village was still in existence in 1621 when there is a record of seven residents.

There is little more to see on visiting the site of the village, which is on Access Land, except to appreciate the choice of the site in a sheltered curve naturally formed in the Downs and to see that the vegetation includes nettles. Nettles are another sign of the presence of man indicating a soil enriched by nitrogen that literally was deposited by man. Nettles can remain for centuries after man has departed.

There is another patch of vegetation alongside the Way at the bottom of the first dip at a point that is marked by an small oblong on the Ordnance Survey Map. The plants are nettles and again they are a sign of man. Here they mark the site of what was once the Fulking Isolation Hospital.

Further on Edburton Hill has three points of interest. In no order of importance, they are Springs Smokery, a motte and bailey castle and the Great Bustard – an ill assorted trio.

Springs lies at the foot of the escarpment and there is a very convenient footpath that leads right down to it. It is, however, best to approach it by road with cheque book and car to carry away the pile that mounts of smoked fish and other goodies. There is no easy way back up to the top of the Downs.

The castle is difficult to see from the Way. Its site can be seen as a slight unevenness in the smooth rounded top up to the right of the Way as one looks up when descending towards the power lines that cross the Way 500 metres beyond the site of the isolation hospital. There is nothing above ground level to show that a castle had been there. The castle would have been Norman but nothing else is known of when exactly it was built or why or who built it. The castle would have been very small but commanding wide views of both Downs and Weald: a look out post or medieval early warning system perhaps.

The motte in a motte and bailey castle is not the moat. Motte comes from the French and that is the direction that the Normans came from although they were originally Norsemen – Vikings – and not French; it means a mound. The French *motte de taupe* meant a mole hill and you can see where the name of the colour came from; wasn't it last year's black some time ago?

There would have been a tower on the mound: at first wooden and later often stone although the castle on Edburton Hill may not have progressed as far as that. The tower would have been the last refuge in the case of attack. There is some evidence that the Norman invasion force brought prefabricated wooden castles with it so that they could be put up as soon as a mound was built.

The bailey was a larger area adjoining the motte surrounded by a wooden palisade in which there would have been the daily living quarters and stabling. Cattle and the local population could have been driven into the baileys of the bigger castles for safety in times of trouble, both cattle and people being possessions of the local lord; one does not now know which that lord considered to be the more valuable.

When clear there is a truly panoramic view of Downs and coast and Weald but it would have been a more than breezy posting at times.

The Great Bustard is long gone from these parts but Edburton Hill used to be one of its haunts until about 1800. The last sighting in Sussex was in 1891 at Pett Levels. Attempts are being made to reintroduce them in Wiltshire using wild birds from abroad but are apparently having mixed success.

They were hunted to extinction in England for sport using greyhounds. Although the Great Bustard is a slow but strong flyer, being one of the largest flying birds, it prefers to run from danger. And it is a big bird. It has a wingspan of up to 2.4 metres (8 feet) and can weigh up to 18 kilograms (40 pounds).

It is becoming rare all over because of over hunting.

Bustard should not be confused with Buzzard.

About 40 years ago, one of the authors on the South Downs wrote that Buzzards *"were not uncommon until the middle of the nineteenth century."* But they are back and quite often can be seen soaring above the Downs with their broad rounded wings, short tails and gull-like cries. Although not as big as the Great Bustard, the Buzzard has a wingspan of about 1 metre (3 feet). See a Buzzard flying and imagine what a sight the Great Bustard must have been.

The Chapel of Lancing College comes into view on this section. In its Victorian Gothic splendour it is another contender for the title of the Cathedral of the Downs. Work started on the chapel in 1868 some 14 years after the first start of work on the first school buildings. It was dedicated in 1911 and there may yet be work to be done.

Lancing College was one of a number of schools that were founded by the Reverend Nathaniel Woodward. These include Lancing, Hurstpierpoint and Ardingly . Each has a great chapel with that at Lancing the best known.

Woodward's declared mission in 1848 was *"to educate the Middle Classes"*. They had then recently been enfranchised by the Reform Act and, no doubt, needed education to teach them how to cast their votes correctly. And elitism was not discouraged in the 19th century. Murray's **Handbook for Travellers in Sussex**, published in 1893, describes the purpose of each establishment although it might be unwise to mention this to any alumni.

Lancing was *"for the education of the upper classes"*: Hurstpierpoint *"for the sons of farmers"*: and Ardingly *"for sons of small traders"*. Hardly a classless society.

Unless it is one of those days when visibility is severely restricted the presence of Shoreham Cement Works in the Adur valley cannot be ignored much as one might wish to. Production of cement ceased in 1991. Since then various proposals have been put forward for the future of the site. These have included, not all at the same time, the inevitable housing, a sports stadium, the Sussex answer to the Eden Project, an artificial ski slope, a hotel, light industrial use with warehousing and waste management including, possibly an incinerator. There are currently no settled plans for its future.

After passing the Youth Hostel on Truleigh Hill one descends into the Adur Valley with Bramber and Steyning where the river gap emerges northwards through the Downs. A glimpse may be caught of a tower with a green conical roof standing alone in the countryside a mile or so to the north of Steyning looking for all the world like an old-fashioned helter skelter that has been marooned far from its attendant fair. This is not the remains of another windmill. Built in 1928 it is the octagonal water tower at Wappingthorne Farm but where once it contained 10,000 tons of water, it now houses people for it has been converted to residential use

The village of Bramber, with the remains of its Norman castle that are rather grander than Edburton, lies just to the north of the Way on the west bank of the river Adur. Bramber was once a rotten parliamentary borough where a total electorate of 18 voters returned two members of parliament – not too much difference from modern interest in elections. It is said that William Wilberforce, who played such a leading part in the abolition of slavery, asked where he was as he was being driven through Bramber in his coach and horses. On being told that it was Bramber, he exclaimed, *"Bramber: Why that's the place I'm Member for!"* – no guesses how many surgeries he held for his electors.

Steyning is just to the west of Bramber. It has many claims to interest and it even has its own saint, St Cuthman, who lived in or about the 8th century AD although, perhaps, to be politically correct it ought to be CE or Common Era

Cuthman was a farm boy who was no stranger to performing a miracle or two. When his father died, he decided to go a-travelling. Being a devoted son he took his mother with him, pushing her ahead of him in a handcart secured by a strap around his shoulders.

The first time the strap broke, that and Cuthman's efforts to mend it were met with derision from hay makers close by. It is not recorded whether mother came tumbling out, which would have heightened the insult, but It is dangerous to laugh at a saint. The Almighty was not pleased and a heavy storm immediately broke out above the field. The crop was destroyed and legend has it that every harvest since then has been endangered in the same way. But that could just be the normal English weather.

When the cart broke down irrevocably, Cuthman took it as a sign from Heaven that he was to stop and stop he did. That was at Steyning where he founded a church.

A possible later occupant of that church for a while was King Ethelwulf, the father of Alfred the Great. Ethelwulf died at Steyning which was then under royal patronage. He was first buried at Steyning but his remains were later transferred to Winchester. There is a broken Saxon coffin lid of stone in the porch of the present church. It is suggested that it came from Ethelwulf's first burial.

Charles Stewart Parnell, the 19th century Irish politician and patriot, whose career collapsed when he was cited as the co-respondent in a divorce case in 1890, married Katherine (otherwise known as Kitty) O'Shea, the woman in the case, in Steyning. The marriage is marked by a plaque on the wall of the building where the wedding took place.

The river Adur in the valley is the third of the four Sussex rivers crossed by the Way. The river seems to have been named not by Celt or Saxon but by mistake. Michael Drayton, a poet in the reign of the first Queen Elizabeth, wrote a monumental topographical poem called **Poly-Olbion** celebrating the beauties and glories of England. The problem was that his geography was a bit off. He thought that the Roman port of *Portus Adurni* (Portsmouth) was at the mouth of the river that he christened the Adur. The up-market name stuck in preference to a variety of names depending upon which village or town on the course of the river you came from.

Not long after having crossed the river, and then the Downs Link with its convenient bench and a fingerpost showing that it is 60 miles to Winchester, there is the not so much deserted as reduced village of Botolphs. There is a hint that it, like the neighbouring village of Coombes under a mile to the south (1.3 kilometres), was a casualty of the Black Death in 1348/49. It is not inconceivable that the plague played a part in its decline but, as so often, economics are a more likely cause when the river receded and left the former fishing port with its river front wharf stranded.

The small typical Downland church of St Botolph founded in Saxon times and containing Saxon work can be seen from the Way and can easily be reached. It is itself evidence of the decline of the village. It was bigger when a northern aisle was added in about 1250. The aisle was removed in the following century when the arches that form part of the present external wall were bricked up. The date is about right for the Black Death so, maybe, that was part of the cause. There are mounds and irregularities close to the church showing where buildings once stood but the manor house still stands. It is now Annington Farm as one ascends the road towards the ridge of the Downs.

St Botolph (or Botolf), is not well known and little is now known about him, although he must have had a popular following. 64 ancient churches were dedicated to him including 3 in London, all of which were rebuilt by Sir Christopher Wren. He appears to have been born in East Anglia, to have founded a monastery, have his church destroyed in Danish invasions, died

in 680 AD and to have had his head and bones shared out amongst various churches. His feast day is 17th June so, perhaps, he ought to be the patron saint of the Annual South Downs Way Walk that is usually in mid-June.

From time to time during this section and the next, including from Chanctonbury Ring itself, the rim of the dew pond close by the Way beyond the Ring and the escarpment in between, the white painted upper works and sails of a windmill can be seen some miles out into the Weald. This is Shipley Windmill and it is a genuine smock mill. It belonged to Hilaire Belloc and stands next to King's Land the home he bought in 1905 and where he lived until his death in 1953.

Most people, in Sussex at least, know the story of the trees of Chanctonbury Ring and how Charles Goring, of Wiston House down below, as a young man in 1760 planted, in his words, *"those twigs"*, carried water up to and tended them until they became established and as an old man saw the beech crown established in early maturity.

It became probably the most famous landmark on the Sussex Downs figuring in countless pictures on walls, in books and on calendars. It suffered badly in the devastation of the great storm in October 1987. It still looks sad today and will take many years to recover. It is called a ring not because of the trees but for the Iron Age fort on and in which the trees were planted. No trees grew in the centre where in 1908 the ruins of a small Roman temple were discovered.

Like many other places along the Downs, Chanctonbury Ring has its legends and, as so often in Sussex, one concerns the Devil. This much is known. If you run round Chanctonbury Ring seven times without stopping you can conjure Him up and He will offer you something that you can eat or drink. There the certainties end. It is not known if this has to be on a special night or nights in the year: whether you have to run forwards or backwards: what He offers you, milk or soup or porridge: what happens if you refuse or accept. Could it be that nobody has returned to tell the tale?

Wiston House can be seen from the front of the escarpment by Chanctonbury Ring to the right amongst trees below. Embezzlement of public funds funded its construction by Sir Thomas Shirley in about 1575. It is, therefore, fitting that the house should now be in government service as a conference centre. Colourful as the career of Sir Thomas may have been, it was eclipsed by those of his sons although as accounts vary it is difficult to be entirely accurate about their exploits. Acting in the Elizabethan bucaneering tradition they tried to restore their family fortunes but without the financial success of some of their near contemporaries.

Sir Thomas, the eldest son, appears to have been the least adventurous but even his career involved privateering in the Mediterranean where he was captured by the Turks. He was released two years later after the intercession of King James I undoubtedly made vastly sweeter by the payment of a huge ransom. He returned home a ruined man and was forced to sell Wiston.

Sir Anthony, the second son, had wider horizons. In 1596 aboard his ship, Bevis of Southampton, he set sail from Plymouth leading a fleet of six other ships. He first attempted to raid southern Africa where he appears to have been driven off by pestilence rather than resistance. Sailing westward across the Atlantic he raided Portuguese and Spanish holdings along the southern American coast and in the West Indies including Jamaica. He returned to England in 1597 in best family tradition and, in the words of Thomas Fuller (1608-1661) in **The History of the Worthies of England**, "*coming off with more honour than profit to himself or the nation...; yet unpartial judgments, who measure not worth by success, justly allow it a prime place amongst the probable (though not prosperous) English Adventures*".

He then turned his attention eastward, arriving at the court of the Shah of Persia on a self- appointed mission to engage the Shah in an alliance against the Turks. Apparently he did engage the attention of the Shah for it seems that the

Shah made him a Prince and appointed him to be the Persian Ambassador to the courts of Europe where he was not always greeted with warmth; the Czar, Boris Godunov, was not impressed but he was welcomed in Rome. He subsequently entered the service of the Spanish crown and, converted to Catholicism, died an ex pat. in Spain without having repaired the family fortunes.

The youngest brother, Sir Robert, had followed his brother to the court of the Shah and succeeded as ambassador to the courts of Europe. He married Teresia, a Christian Circassian lady of high degree, and he adopted Persian clothing. In the words of Fuller, "*He much affected to appear in* forreign Vestes*; and, as if his* Clothes *were his limbs, accounted himself never ready till he had something of the Persian Habit about him*". Their portraits by Vandyk can be seen at Petworth House. Robert died in 1628, another ex pat.

Two and a half miles to the south of Chanctonbury Ring there is another Iron Age hill fort – Cissbury Ring. Far more impressive than Chanctonbury, it has been described as, "*the most formidable earth fort on any English chalk hilltop apart from Maiden Castle in Dorset*". If it is still impressive today after 2,000 years of neglect and weathering and wear and tear, how impressive must it have been in its heyday when its ditches were clear of the accumulated dirt and rubbish of centuries and its white chalk ramparts crowned by a revetment of some 8 to 12,000 timbers set on end each of 6 to 9 inches in diameter and at least 15 feet long.

The hill top was in use long before the fort was built. There are mines up there, possibly more than 200, where late Neolithic (New Stone Age: 3500-2000 BC) people dug for flints. It was the Weald with the iron industry that became a leading industrial area in 16th, 17th and 18th centuries AD but an earlier industrial zone was along the South Downs. Arthur Beckett in **The Spirit of the Downs** refers to Cissbury being known as "*the Flint Sheffield*" for flint, a very hard rock, has the property of flaking that allows it to produce very sharp edges and be shaped into a variety of tools and weapons.

Although there was no shortage of flints on the surface, those that were exposed became harder to work. The better flints were mined. Using picks of deer antlers and shovels of animal shoulder blades, shafts twenty feet deep were sunk, some with galleries radiating out from them. A poignant reminder of those people is the skeleton of a young woman that was found in one of the mines on Cissbury Hill in the course of archaeological excavations; but no one knows whether she fell or was pushed.

Below the escarpment at Chanctonbury Ring there is an indication of the diversity of Sussex and how quickly it can change. In a matter of moments one can move to a completely different landscape. On the Downs one is up on the rounded chalk hills but almost immediately below at Rock Common there are the sand diggings that are the last signs of the southern arm of the Greensand Ridge that runs like a giant horseshoe within the arms of the North and South Downs.

The sailless windmill below, on the edge of Rock Common, Rock Mill, was the last home of John Ireland, the composer. He died in 1962 and is buried in the churchyard at Shipley a few miles to the north in view of the Downs that he loved. He was inspired by the Downs and one of his compositions, a piano piece, **Amberley Wild Brooks**, celebrates an another aspect of the diverse landscape of Sussex that will be seen below the Downs in the next section.

Close to him now lies Norah Kirby, his housekeeper and companion. She died twenty years later in 1982 but it was not until 1985 that she was buried in Shipley churchyard. She had spent most of the remainder of her life furthering the reputation of John Ireland and his music but in 1982 she fell ill. She went into a nursing home near Margate where she died some months later having, in the meantime, made a will leaving her entire estate to the owners of the home.

Her friends rallied; the planned cremation was halted and her assets withheld from distribution. The nursing home owners were investigated for theft and the administration of poisonous substances. They were never convicted but the will in their favour was set aside. After over two years the body was released from cold storage and finally laid to rest at Shipley.

About 400 metres after passing the dewpond on Chanctonbury Hill particular care should be taken to follow the Way. The track stretches broad and inviting ahead downhill but the Way goes right. Miss it and you can be taken quite a way out from where you want to be.

It's a golden rule never to blindly follow the people in front but we have all done it. They may be on the South Downs Way but there are alternatives. They may know where they are going but it's not the same way that you want to go: or they may also have missed the Way. And we've all done that too.

Washington to Whiteways

"They sell good Beer at Haslemere
And under Guildford Hill.
At little Cowfold as I've been told
A beggar may drink his fill:
There is a good brew in Amberley too,
And by the bridge also;
But the swipes they take in at the Washington Inn
Is the very best beer I know."

Hillaire Belloc
(1870-1953)

Above is the first verse of Hilaire Belloc's **West Sussex Drinking Song** and the last lines cover much of the country in the first part of this stage. The Washington Inn is the Frankland Arms where the previous stage may have been ended. The Way crosses the River Arun by a footbridge close to Amberley with Houghton Bridge just to the south where there is, indeed, a pub called The Bridge Inn. No challenges are issued to walkers to test the delights of all the places mentioned by Belloc. He had a long lifetime to do that. Born in 1870 he died 1953. The 50th anniversary of his death was commemorated in 2003 year by events across Sussex.

The Rev Parish's **Dictionary of the Sussex Dialect** ignores the word, 'swipes' but Tony Wales in **Sussex as she wus spoke** (2000) defines it as "*Light beer*".

The Way passes the latest in a succession of large barns on the crest of the ridge where many a walker has sheltered to eat their sandwiches. A far better example is in the group of buildings below at Manor Farm next to Sullington Church. At 115 feet (35 metres) long it doesn't quite match the grandeur of the 170 feet (52 metres) of the barn at Alciston (remember AHLSTON) near Alfriston, but it is impressive in its own right. There is a date of 1685 on one of its timbers but that is probably when it was renewed and not when the barn was built. Like many other big barns it has been called a tithe barn but probably was not. Like Alciston it was probably needed to take 100% from its owner's estate; not just a tenth from parishioners.

The little church close by contains Saxon work and holds a life-size 13th century stone memorial of a knight in chain mail. It is thought that it might be Sir William de Covert, whose family once held the manor, and that it could be the oldest stone monument in Sussex. It is very battered but who wouldn't be after eight hundred years.

The hills just to the south (left going towards Winchester) are first, Blackpatch Hill (not to be confused with Blackcap near Lewes) and then Harrow Hill.

The Ordnance Survey map shows that there are earthworks and flint mines at the top of Harrow Hill. What it does not tell is that Harrow Hill is reputed to be the last home in England of the Pharisees – the Sussex name for fairies of the magical variety. There have not been confirmed sightings for many a year. Even the photographs that captivated the great Arthur Conan Doyle in the 1920s are said to have been a hoax – but were they?

Perhaps the Pharisees, like Tolkien's elves from Lórien, have left and, probably centuries ago. Richard Corbet, a poet at the time of the reign of the first Queen Elizabeth, suspected as much. He wrote:

> "But now, alas, they all are dead;
> Or gone beyond the seas;
> Or further for religion fled,
> Or else they take their ease."

But, who knows, they may still be about. Arthur Beckett believed that "*the modern scientific mind has made the fairies shy*", and that "*they appear only to poets, country folk and little children, who are wiser than we are*". If they are there, those wearing green will have to keep an extra sharp look out. Green is the special colour of the fairies and they think that the wearing of that colour is an invitation to them and that you want to join them. But remember that the fairy world has its own space and time and that when you emerge, if you ever do, you will be the same but those who were of your age will have advanced many years beyond.

There is a relic of the Second World War in the corner of a field between 300 and 400 metres to the south of the Way. It can be reached at TQ072122 by a short diversion from the Way over public rights of way. It is the rusting hull of a Mark II Churchill Tank dating from the days when hereabouts was almost Canadian territory. The bullet-riddled remains are far from glorifying war. They are a compelling reminder of the conditions under which soldiers of all sides fought. Surprisingly small compared to the mammoths that seem to

loom across our television screens now, these tanks carried a crew of five: driver, co-driver, radio operator, gunner and commander, although each had to be prepared to fill in for another at a moment's notice. They were surrounded by personal equipment, rations and a highly combustible mixture of ammunition for the guns including the large calibre main armament and fuel, all in a cramped space. They knew that a moment's inattention or exposure over a ridge could mean instant annihilation by enemy fire. The solution was if possible to be 'hull down': the driver to manoeuvre the tank so that it was sheltered behind the ridge with only the head of the tank commander, sitting on or in the turret, appearing briefly above the ridge.

It is to such men as these that we have the freedom that enables us to enjoy the wide and open freedom of the Downs.

Continuing southwards on either of the paths that converge at the tank will, in about a mile, take you to Lee Farm. Although an old established farm there is no ancient farmhouse nestling in a sheltered spot. Lee Farm became another casualty of the Second World War when it too was used for target practice.

The old thatched building was replaced by a modern building on a different site after the War. There is a tradition that Lee Farm was once a leper colony. No documentary evidence has been found to support that but it could be so. The track that runs from Lee Farm to Burpham is called the Lepers' Way and there is a 'squint', sometimes called a lepers' window, at Burpham Church; a low window to give those outside the church a view inside especially those not permitted to enter the church.

The hills that are seen on the northern 'horizon' are not the North Downs. They are the northern arm of the Greensand Ridge the southern end of which we saw below Chanctonbury Ring. They lie in front of and here mask the North Downs which is not surprising as one of those hills is Leith Hill in Surrey which at 967 feet (295 metres) is the highest point in south-east England.

It is possible to make out the tower on top of Leith Hill: for some of us with the aid of binoculars. The story goes that Richard Hull, an 18th century philosopher who lived at Leith Hill Place, was granted permission by his landlords to build a tower on the top of the hill that brought the height to over 1,000 feet and thus created a mountain: 1,000 feet then being considered to be the proper height for a mountain.

But back to Sussex: the hill to the left at the start of the range is Blackdown which is the highest point in Sussex and where Tennyson built Aldworth, the home in where he spent his last years hoping for a quiet life after being driven from the Isle of Wight by the Victorian version of the cult of celebrity. Is it the grumpy old man that observes that celebrities had more to celebrate then.

A quiet, not to say silent life, is experienced by the glider pilots who take off from Parham Airfield below once they have been cast off by the aeroplane that has released them from the ground. For a while they soar above the Downs; then they are gone. They head to the west around Cheltenham or the north about Oxford. And they fly back again: not for them the indignity of being pulled back in a trailer after the freedom of the skies.

Seen close to the airfield, Parham is another of those great houses that lie beneath the escarpment of the Downs. Simon Jenkins rates it five stars and sums it up as "*a house of magic*". It too with its collection of fine paintings and embroidery is open to the public at various times during the year. Built of local stone under a Horsham Stone roof, it was begun in 1577 in the reign of the first Queen Elizabeth by Thomas Palmer, the first stone being laid by his two year old son. It is built in the traditional 'E' pattern that some say commemorates the E of Elizabeth. That was probably purely coincidental as the E-Plan predates Elizabeth's succession to the throne but doubtless there were those who took the opportunity to claim that their inspiration was from Gloriana herself. Parham was sold to the Bysshopp family in 1601 in whose possession it remained until 1922. It has been owned by the Pearsons since then.

The house is surrounded by a deer park where the deer still roam at large. Parham Church stands amongst the trees 200 metres to the south of the house. The church was once amid a village but, possibly due to an extension of the deer park, the villagers moved away to nearby Rackham. The houses were demolished leaving the church isolated but still in use. At some stage in the 18th or early 19th century high box pews were installed including the squire's pew with its own entrance from the outside and, height of luxury, a fireplace.

The hamlet of Rackham lies at the foot of Rackham Hill between Parham and Amberley. All the guide books seem to miss Rackham but it serves us as a link to Arthur Rackham (1867-1939), the well known illustrator, perhaps best known for his illustrations to fairy tales. He lived at Houghton House close to Amberley between 1920 and 1930.

To the south west there are distant views of Arundel Castle standing guard over what was once an important route inland along the River Arun. At one time it was possible to reach London along the canals and navigations starting from the mouth of the Arun at Littlehampton. Many parts of that system are still navigable by small craft and efforts are continually being made to extend the usable stretches.

Arundel Castle was also the model for Gormengast in Mervyn Peake's Titus novels. Mervyn Peake lived at Burpham which is opposite Arundel across the Arun and he is buried in the churchyard at Burpham.

The river is called the Arun after the town of Arundel. The river has an older Celtic name commemorated in the name of Tarrant Street in Arundel along which many of us have passed to Pegler's boot shop – (if we have any money after visiting their other shops on the way). It became the Arun in about the 1200s.

There is a theory that the name 'Arundel' comes from the hoarhound, a plant that was once abundant in the valley, so that it was known hoarhound dale (or the Anglo Saxon rendering of that which does sound a bit more like Arundel) and that may be the true reason.

The more interesting tradition says that Arundel comes from 'Hirondelle', the French word for a swallow. There is a swallow on the arms of Arundel and Hirondelle was also the name of the horse of the legendary giant Bevis of Hampton. He was the warder of the gatehouse at Arundel Castle for the Earls of Arundel who allowed him rations of a whole ox and two hogsheads of beer each week. You would not want him to prolong a stay with you for too long.

His size was gargantuan and is celebrated in the name Bevis Thumb which at 210 feet (64 metres) is the longest known long barrow in Sussex. It is on the Downs near Compton which is close to the border with Hampshire and about one and a half miles (2.5 kilometres) south of the South Downs Way.

Less than a mile to the south of the Way at Amberley Mount there is, where the shoulder of the Downs sweeps down to North Stoke and the Arun Valley, a holding, now in ruins, marked on the Ordnance Survey as 'Canada'. It is tempting to think that it was named for the Canadians who trained here during World War II but the name goes back further than that. Names such as 'Canada' were often used to describe a holding or field that was remote, for the country of Canada was then a remote place and this holding is not exactly at the hub of things.

At the 1881 census, 1 Canada was occupied by William Moulding, a shepherd, and his wife and their seven children aged between 10 years and 3 months; next door at No. 2 there was George Curtis, an agricultural labourer, and his wife with two sons aged 18 and 16 and a step daughter of 12. In his book **Spirit of the Downs**, originally published in 1909, Arthur Beckett comments upon the overcrowded conditions of some of those who lived on the Downs: *"The cottage … contained two bedrooms and two lower rooms; and, on occasions, the bedrooms were occupied by no less than seven persons, including a mother and a grown-up daughter. In one bedroom were two beds, the mother and daughter slept in one, and the father and two sons in the other. The second bedroom contained one bed, which was occupied by the two remaining men: a son of the family and his uncle, who was on a visit to his relatives."*

Arthur Beckett does also say that this *"state of affairs (was) probably exceptional"*, but there was a total of nine in Mr and Mrs Moulding's family in a space that if it was larger cannot have been have been much greater.

To the north the beautiful village of Amberley stands close to the banks of the river Arun opposite the end of the ridge as it descents into the Arun valley.

When the river floods, as it sometimes does, Amberley is then on the banks of the Arun but, due to its height, is never in or under the river although it has been said that the women of Amberley are born with webbed feet. Why the same condition does not affect the males of the population is not recorded: a reluctance to make the acquaintance of water perhaps.

Being in Sussex, that land of contradictions, Amberley has its examples. The castle is not a castle and the Wild Brooks, may not mean what the words appear to say.

The castle is not a castle as technically it is a fortified manor house. It stands on land that was given in 682 AD to St Wilfrid who brought Christianity to the South Saxons and who it is said taught them to fish and so averted starvation from the land. It was a Bishop of Chichester, Ralph Luffa, who in about 1100 AD built the Manor House much of which still survives within the walls. It was he who was also responsible for building Amberley Church and the first Chichester Cathedral.

The licence to crenellate (fortify) that the King alone could authorise was granted by King Richard II in 1377 and the walls that can now be seen were built. Opinion seems to be divided over the need for fortification. Was it fear of foreign invasion or uprisings by the local population? Perhaps a mixture of both: as we have seen the French were never backward in raiding up the river valleys and it was also a period of domestic social unrest. The church, to which the 'castle' still belonged, was a rich and powerful institution not wholly loved: indeed, a few years later in 1381, Archbishop Sudbury, the Archbishop of Canterbury, was murdered during the Peasants' Revolt of which Wat Tyler was one of the leaders.

Both threats bypassed Amberley. The 'castle' suffered its worst damage in the English Civil War. Although the curtain wall was not badly affected much of the interior was destroyed. After that history passed it by. It is now a very fine hotel and it too has its stars in *England's Thousand Best Houses*.

Beyond Amberley the quiet flatness of Amberley Wild Brooks stretches to the north. Often impassable in winter they are a haven for birds and a place of international importance. They are one of the surviving wetlands but only just. In the 1970s they were the subject of contention between two government departments. What is now English Nature wished to preserve them for the nation; the Ministry of Agriculture wanted to grant money for an 'improvement scheme' that would have led to their destruction. Fortunately English Nature won.

It seems almost churlish to intrude on the tranquillity of the Wild Brooks, usually only disturbed by the honking of geese, by an over pedantic analysis of the name when it all seems so obvious. The thick volume, *Place Names of Sussex*, offers that here "*Wild could mean uncultivated*". The alternative is that 'Wild' is a corruption of 'Weald' and that the meaning is that these are the brooks in the Weald. But to avoid confusing the issue too far we will presume that 'wild' means the area that we call The Weald and not the other alternative meanings of the word.

It is not entirely appropriate to say that we are on firmer ground with 'Brooks' but there is more certainty of its meaning. It is one of those contrary Sussex words. In Sussex it does not mean small streams but water meadows that were particularly important where meadows for grazing were in short supply.

In the end it may not really matter what a place is called or how and why it got its name. A place and sense of place transcend a name, although knowing the detail can add a sense of intimacy and acquaintance with a place. It may be, however, that it really is part, as Hilaire Belloc pointed out, of Adam's plan to give Sussex "*names of a sort that give fools to think*".

The church at the village of Bury on the bank of the Arun can be seen as you descend Amberley Mount and also as you ascend the other side of the valley.

Bury House in the village was the country home of John Galsworthy. In 1926 he was looking for a house in the south coast area that would primarily be a home for his nephew but where he would have a suite of rooms and that he would finance to £3,000. They found nothing that suited. On the point of despair they visited the agents in Pulborough. There was nothing of the sort that they were looking for. There was a house in Tudor style with 15 bedrooms that had just come on the market. It was not what they wanted but some chance made them go to view it. First sight was not impressive. They nearly turned back but having come that far they felt that they ought to take a closer look and went through the gate. Galsworthy turned the corner of the house, saw the Downs and said, *"This is the place"* without having set foot inside the house. And so it was. They returned to Pulborough where Galsworthy secured it by offering the full asking price of £9,000, three times his intended budget.

Galsworthy was already a famous author when he came to Bury. He finished the chronicles of the Forsyte family there. His ashes were scattered on Bury Hill.

The final stage coming down into the Arun Valley is along High Titten that passes Amberley Working Museum. The site of the museum has its place in world history and the saving of mankind. As those addicted to international affairs will know it was here that Grace Jones sacrificed her all, or was that earlier in the film – anyway here she gave her life to enable James Bond, alias Roger Moore, to go on to defeat the villainies of Max Zorin whose evil plan was to flood Silicon Valley and take command of the world through sole control of the computer industry. It was here that the atom bomb was placed to trigger the devastation of Silicon Valley.

Those who have seen the film **From a View to a Kill** may be forgiven for expecting to see the city of San Francisco just over the next rise as James Bond did dangling below the airship that lifted him from here – for the unbelievers, it was firmly suspended from a very tall crane at the time.

At the bottom of High Titten where it meets the road there is a signpost. This shows that Eastbourne is now 50 miles back along the Way; Winchester lies 51 miles ahead.

As you may know there is a pub called the George and Dragon up the hill from Houghton Bridge: an old timber framed building. Just over 350 years ago on 15th October 1651, a party of four horsemen stopped at the door and, without dismounting, took a quick meal of bread and beer plus a couple of ox tongues that Colonel Gunter, one of the party, had filched from his sister's kitchen at her house near Hambledon where they had spent the previous night.

With Colonel Gunter was Lord Wilmot, Robert Shaw who was Lord Wilmot's servant, and a groom that the wanted notices described as, "*a tall, black man six feet two inches high*" – black here meaning having a dark complexion.

The "*tall, black man*" was Charles II, then uncrowned, seeking an escape route out of the country after defeat at the battle of Worcester.

From Houghton, the party went on to Arundel and Bramber. They had close encounters with Roundhead soldiers at both places. The king finally took ship from Shoreham, the coal-brig Surprise, owned and commanded by Nicholas Tettersell, and went into exile until, 9 years later in 1660, he was restored to the throne and crowned.

Although Charles II was not renowned for gratitude, after the Restoration he did reward those who had helped him during his escape. Captain Tettersell sailed the Surprise up the Thames and anchored her off the Palace of Whitehall to put her on show to the public and to make sure that he was not overlooked. The ship was refitted and taken into the Royal Navy and Captain Tettersell was appointed as an officer in the Navy. In 1663 he was also granted a pension of £100 a year to be paid for a period of 99 years first to him and then to his family after his death.

There is a choice of ways ahead for those using the car park at Whiteways as a staging post. The purists will wish to follow the South Downs Way itself crossing the Arun by the footbridge that was installed in 1995 and climbing to the main road (A29) past Coombe Wood. If you follow this route take care not to miss the first footpath to the left about 300 metres after the A29 to take you down towards the location of the car park.

For the less devout a left turn at the bottom of High Titten will take you down to Houghton Bridge. Here there is The Bridge Inn on one side of the road and tea rooms overlooking the river on the other. Following the road across the bridge and up the hill will take you past the George and Dragon to meet the Monarch's Way that leads directly to the car park.

The Monarch's Way, which has already been crossed on the way up from the Adur to Chanctonbury Ring and is encountered again on Old Winchester Hill, is long distance foot path 610 miles (981 kilometres) long from Worcester to Shoreham-by-Sea. It commemorates that escape by Charles II including the celebrated occasion when he hid in an oak tree from those hunting him: the original Royal Oak.

Whiteways to Cocking

"To this green hill something dream-like clings,
Where day by day the little blunt sheep graze,
Threading the tussocks and the toad-stool rings,
Nosing the barrows of the olden days.
An air drifts here that's sweet of sea and grass,
And down the coombe-side living colour glows
Spring, Summer, Fall, the chasing seasons pass
To Winter, even lovelier than those."

John Galsworthy
(1867-1933)
From ***Bury Hill***

The A29 marks a significant change in the outward character of the Downs. To the east there was the open, rolling country traditionally associated with the Downs. To the west the hundreds of feet depth of underlying chalk remain the same but now there is much more woodland. This gives a different dimension to the Downs. There is almost an optical illusion with the trees on the skyline giving a scale by which the sense of great height above the Weald now seems much smaller. There are still long, wide views to be had but, not until we reach Hampshire, the continuous 360° sweep that has gone before. The open spaces were not always so. Those, in Kipling's words, "*Bare slopes where chasing shadows skim*", were once wooded too. Archaeological evidence shows that the chalk grassland is not natural to the Downs but developed over several thousand years following clearances by man starting in the Neolithic period (4000 BC onwards) through the succeeding Bronze and Iron Ages to be probably almost complete by the time the Roman Empire governed Britain.

Clearances on the Downs did not stop in Roman times, although some later clearances were of grassland, not woodland. In the early stages of this section there is in Houghton Forest the oddly named Denture a kilometre to the south of the Way. Denture is a name that also occurs elsewhere in Sussex. It is the result of a misspelling for 'dencher' or 'densher' which is a corruption (or Sussex version) of Devonshire. A mid 17th century practice in Devonshire for reclaiming unimproved ground involved paring off and burning the turf and ploughing in the ashes to fertilise the ground. Before the 17th century the turf of the sheep walks on the Downs was strictly protected but new fodder crops introduced about that time were better foodstuffs and consequently less grassland was needed for the sheep and could be cleared and used for other crops.

The Romans built it but it was the Saxons who named it Stane Street – the road or street made from stone, the stone being the slabs of stone that were used to pave its surface: at least in parts. Stone was not the only surfacing material used by the Romans.

We do not know what the Romans called it or even if it had anything less prosaic than a number. It is not mentioned in the list of Roman roads called the Antonine Itinerary; many are not. Archaeological evidence suggests that it was probably built between 60 and 70 AD but it could have been earlier and closer to the invasion of Britain under the Emperor Claudius in 43 AD.

It is more than probable that the road did not much echo to the tramp of the legions or the sounds of battle as Romans were harried by the native inhabitants fighting for their homeland and freedom. It was probably used mainly for trade, the Imperial postal service and to carry corn from the rich farmlands of southern Sussex to London and elsewhere to feed the Roman Empire. The Roman 'invasion' was almost certainly welcomed in Sussex where the local king, Cogidubnus, remained in power. There had long been trading links across the Channel and the benefits of Roman civilisation with its central heating and hot baths were, no doubt, appreciated in the British climate, at least by the ruling classes and those who could afford them.

A signpost stands on Bignor Hill by Stane Street. The southwards arm points to Noviomagus, the Roman name for Chichester, where Stane Street begins; northwards lies the end of the road at Londinium (London). The signpost also shows that on the way to London is the village of Bignor at the foot of the escarpment.

Bignor is famous for its Roman Villa that was discovered in 1811 in the course of ploughing. Fortunately antiquarian interest prevailed over agricultural produce and its fine mosaics showing Ganymede, gladiatorial combat, dancing girls and Venus, amongst others, together with part of the central heating system (hypocaust) were saved.

Less well known, certainly at the time, is the part that Bignor Manor played in the Second World War. Between 1941 and 1944 it was the home of Major Anthony Bertram and his wife Barbara. They provided a safe house for French secret intelligence agents to wait for their moonlit flights by Lysander aircraft into occupied France from Tangmere on the other side of the Downs and to be received when, and if, they came back again. More than 200 agents, men and women, passed through the house. Only a handful knew its real purpose: the cover story was that it was a convalescent home for French Officers. And the 'guests' were never told its exact location so that they could not reveal it under torture.

Amidst all this family life continued with the children Tim and Nicky plus Duff-the-Dog, Peter-the-cat, two rabbits, about twelve hens, two hives of bees and Caroline-the-goat after whom a clandestine operation was named and for whom low flying over Bignor was forbidden when she was in confinement.

Beware the dragon whichever way you come or go to Bignor Hill. Not as well known as some of the Sussex dragons and more worm like than the more conventional fire breathing variety, it coils itself about the hill. The marks of its coils can be seen round the hill although there are some who would have you believe that they are but sheep tracks.

Bearing this caveat in mind, if you turn south and head down Stane Street instead of heading on westwards to Winchester, you come to a village called Eartham. William Huskisson MP lived there in the early 19th century. He was a quite distinguished politician in his day but his lasting claim to fame is, perhaps, that he was the first fatality in a railway accident when he was run over in 1830 by the locomotive, Rocket, at the opening of the Liverpool-Manchester Railway.

His demise is celebrated in verse by a Mr T Baker in his poem, **The Steam Engine**, quoted in an anthology, **The World's Worst Poetry** – true: published by Prion Books in 2002 at p30…

> *"The trains are stopp'd, the mighty chiefs of flame*
> *To quench their thirst the crystal waters claim;*
> *While from their post the great in crowds alight,*
> *When, by a line-train, in its hasty flight,*
> *Through striving to avoid it, Huskisson*
> *By unforeseen mischance was over-run.*
> *That stroke, alas! was death in shortest time;*
> *Thus fell the great financier in his prime!*
> *This fatal chance not only caused delay,*
> *But damped the joy erst had crown'd the day."*

It goes on. Any thoughts about the wrong kind of passengers would be in the worst possible taste.

Sometime in the 1920s a number of writers met in a symposium called **Britain's Most Lovely Walk**. Not much else is known about it except that Hilaire Belloc's contribution went as follows: "*It is difficult to choose, but I think on the whole the most remarkable eight miles I know, which can only be seen walking or riding were those on the Stane Street, from near Eartham in Sussex to Hardham. Since the Nore Wood was cut down in the war only the last part of it, from Gumber Corner onwards preserves the old character. If this destruction has too much spoilt these eight miles, then my next choice would be the walk from Burpham , close by, over the downs to Storrington by way of Parham house.*"

Woods now grow again.

In July 2003 a plaque was unveiled at Gumber Farm, close to the remains of Stane Street, to mark the 50th anniversary of Belloc's death in 1953.

Noviomagus, the new market, and southern terminal of Stane Street, later to become Cissa's ceastre (Cissa's fort) or Chichester, can be seen on the Coastal Plain beyond the Downs with the spire of the cathedral standing plain, unobscured by tall buildings. Chichester is primarily a Georgian town with medieval town walls on foundations of Roman walls. The only sign of its Norman castle is what is left of the motte in Priory Park. No traces of a stone keep having been built on its summit have been found although there are records of it still in use, then as a gaol, in 1198.

Built on the site of an earlier Saxon church, the cathedral was started in the early 1100s and work continued over the next centuries. The spire that provides such a clear landmark is a replica. The original spire "*telescoped in a spectacular way in 1861"* (Nairn and Pevsner) It was replaced by Sir George Gilbert Scott, the eminent Victorian architect, whose work included such well known landmarks as the Albert Memorial and St Pancras Station in London.

Chichester had its place on the medieval pilgrimage circuit. It had, and still has, its own saint, St Richard, who is also the patron saint of Sussex. He was appointed to be Bishop of Chichester in 1244 against the wishes of the English King, Henry III, whom we met briefly being defeated at Lewes. A humble and holy man, St Richard was cut off from the revenues of his office by the King but carried out his duties virtually penniless until the King relented two years later. He died in 1253. His feast day is 3rd April. He came to symbolise the resistance of the spiritual to civilian power. It is little wonder that an early act at the Reformation was King Henry VIII, that most autocratic of monarchs, ordering the destruction of St. Richard's shrine at Chichester. Way to the south, right on the coast, a glimmer of white can sometimes be seen. This is not white cliffs but Butlins at Bognor.

The windmill that can be seen towards the south is Halnaker Mill. Belloc's poem **Halnaker Mill** was written when the mill was in ruin and expresses despair at the condition of England. The sweeps had fallen and there is a sense of desolation in the final verse:

"Ha'nacker's down and England's done.
Wind and thistle for pipe and dancers
And never a ploughman under the Sun.
Never a ploughman. Never a one."

But as you may be able to see, the sweeps are back on Halnaker Mill and we are still here 80 plus years later.

It is not that long ago that Piltdown Man was unmasked as an impostor. He does live on in the text books as an object lesson but Boxgrove, just to the south west of Halnaker, has redeemed Sussex archaeology and confirmed the county's long continuity of human occupation when Boxgrove Man, or is it Woman, was discovered in the early 1980s: although probably male, the section of tibia that was found is insufficient to determine sex but does indicate a height of about 1.8 metres (5 feet 10 inches) and a weight of 80 kilos (176 pounds or 12 stone 8 pounds). He, or she, was in the neighbourhood somewhere between 524,000 and 478,000 years ago. Life was not altogether smooth. In the words of Miles Russell (**Prehistoric Sussex** 2002), *"The large wolf-like gnawing evident across the human tibia from Boxgrove provides sufficient warning that early humans were not necessarily at the top of the food chain"*.

Care needs to be taken when crossing the A285 at Littleton Farm from which the Way climbs up Littleton Down. Hiding in the woods on the southerly side is Crown Tegleaze. At 253 metres (830 feet) it is the highest point on the Sussex Downs. It is not now the highest passed by the Way since it was extended over the Hampshire Border to take in Butser Hill. 'Teg' is a Sussex word for a yearling sheep and the whole means a right to pasture sheep.

Having achieved the climb, the Way enters woodland that masks views northwards including sight of Lavington House just below the escarpment: now Seaford College. It is not one of the great houses but it and the little church next to it, now the school's chapel, are reminders the convoluted church politics of the 19th century.

If you look at the Ordnance Survey Map you may notice Seaford College and Bishops Clump on Duncton Down about a kilometre to the south east of the College. The Bishop was Samuel Wilberforce, the son of William Wilberforce whom we met as MP of Bramber. Samuel Wilberforce was Bishop of Winchester, after having been Bishop of Oxford, but he was also a considerable landowner in this area. What is now Seaford College was Lavington House and surrounding land then belonged to the Wilberforce family. He had been destined for great things within the Church of England but his ultimate rise was impeded by church politics. He died in 1875 falling from his horse following a heart attack.

Although there is a memorial to him in Winchester Cathedral, his pastoral staff is in that little church and he is buried in the churchyard outside. Nearby is the grave of his sister-in-law, Caroline Manning. Some years after she died her husband, Henry, who had also shown great promise as a member of the clergy of the Church of England, converted to Roman Catholicism. He became one of the great 19th century figures of that faith: a prince of the church: Cardinal Manning, Archbishop of Westminster.

Cocking to Queen Elizabeth Park

"Today I want the sky,
The tops of the high hills,
Above the last man's house,
His hedges, and his cows,
Where, if I will, I look
Down even on sheep and rook,
And of all things that move
See buzzards only above."

Edward Thomas
(1878-1917)
From *The Lofty Sky*

There was a large, white spherical object just under the skyline to the left of the Way as you view the hill ahead from the car park where the Way crosses the main road. 'Was' because although the object is still there, it has lost its pristine whiteness. It is becoming weathered and is under attack by those who feel the need to preserve their immortality by the carving of their initials. It is the first, or last, of a series of chalk stones created by the internationally known British artist, Andy Goldsworthy, along a five mile trail stretching from Cocking to West Dean for one of a number of art projects in West Sussex for 2002. Each stone is approximately 6 to 7 feet in diameter.

Andy Goldsworthy is an environmental artist. Materials to hand in a chosen location are used to capture the essence of a place and to reflect the local area. Here it is the chalk from which the Downs are formed. The great mass of the chalk is largely covered and although the covering is thin, the chalk can still look out of place when it is revealed.

It is from the chalk ball that the grandstand at Goodwood can be seen. It is on the skyline away to the south with, to its right, the outline of St. Roches's Hill topped by the earthworks of the Iron Age fort of the Trundle that cannot be seen at this distance and the radio masts that can.

The hill is called St. Roche's Hill from the chapel dedicated to St. Roche that stood on top of the hill from sometime between 1275 and 1400, until the Reformation in the mid 1500s. There is a mound that is said to be the site of the chapel. St Roche (otherwise Roch, Rocco or Rock) was French, lived between about 1350 and 1380 and spent much of his time making pilgrimages. Of the miracles attributed to him was curing those afflicted by the plague and, when himself suffering from the plague, being fed in the woods by a dog. In an age when many for one reason or another went on pilgrimage the length and breadth of Europe, it is not inconceivable that a local man himself went on pilgrimage, became inspired by the story of St Roche and built the chapel to him on return to England. Many of the English churches dedicated to St. James were built by rich landowners after having made the great pilgrimage to the shrine of St. James at Compostela, either from devotion or as a symbol of their achievement.

The Devil's Jumps are not like the treasure that He moves away when you look in the right place but they, and the way into them, are easy to miss, particularly coming from the Winchester direction. Once found, the information board at the site tells us that these barrows are the best example of a Bronze Age barrow cemetery on the South Downs and that is not hard to believe. There are five main barrows between 2 and 5 metres (6½ and 16½ feet) in height and 27 and 34 metres (88½ and 111½ feet) in diameter: other barrows previously met on the Way pale into insignificance. But this is a rich area for barrows. There is Bevis Thumb a bit further on and about 4 miles (6 kilometres) southwards there are the Devils' Humps on the top of Bow Hill from which Uppark and Harting Down can be seen.

Bow Hill stands above Kingley Vale that has one of the finest yew forests in western Europe including a grove of gnarled trees that were ancient when the Normans came to England in 1066 and could have been there when the Romans arrived a thousand years before that.

We are often told that we always have a choice in life. This may not always be essentially true but on this section there is. The path straight ahead lies over Beacon Hill which, at 242 metres (794 feet), gives commanding views of the land below the Downs. The route over Beacon Hill is a public footpath but the official South Downs Way, which remains a bridleway, now diverts in a dog leg to pass close by Telegraph House before rejoining the westward progression just beyond Beacon Hill. Some of the more thirsty may choose to make a somewhat longer diversion to take in the Royal Oak at Hooksway. Sometimes those who escort the annual South Downs Walk promoted by the West Sussex County Council have the choice removed from them when they draw the short straw and have to visit the pub to make sure that none of the walkers gets left behind, but that is one of the penalties of duty.

If you are going in the Winchester direction and want to visit the Royal Oak, take the official South Downs Way route instead of going over Beacon Hill and, when the Way turns sharp right, continue straight ahead downhill to Hooksway. There is no need to retrace your steps on leaving the pub although the purist may wish to do so. The easiest way back is to continue ahead uphill on the road that runs past the pub and take the bridleway on the right about 250 metres beyond the pub. It can be easy to miss, particularly when the fingerpost is obscured by vegetation. If you reach the "T" junction with the road at the top of the hill you have gone too far and will have to backtrack about 150 metres looking for the turning that is now to the left. Take that and continue ahead, forking to the left in about one kilometre to go past  Telegraph House and then on to rejoin the Way.

The Royal Oak dates from the 16th century or, possibly, earlier. Alfred Ainger took the pub over from his father in 1907. They were not a long line of Sussex innkeepers or even of Sussex country stock. Alfred was a real Cockney, born close to the sound of Bow Bells. His father brought the family south, in Alfred's words, when "*old 'Jack the Ripper' was about in 1887*". Alfred was at the pub until 1971 when he retired aged about 89 years old. The facilities that are now taken for granted were some time in coming. Electric light was a long time ahead, Alfred confiding, towards the end of his occupation, that, "*people come from all over to see my oil lamps*". And, when asked by a Midhurst magistrate on an application for the renewal of his licence about the provision of lavatory facilities, replied, "*I've got nine acres, sir*".

We are these days becoming used to wedding ceremonies being conducted in licensed buildings other than churches, chapels or registry offices. Long before that was permitted a wedding, albeit somewhat informal, took place in the Royal Oak in 1910. A regular customer, Eli King, had been keeping company with a young woman who would accompany him to the pub. One evening another 'regular' named Page suggested that it was time they married and that he would officiate for a fee of two gallons of beer. The couple agreed. With a clean towel tucked into his shirt collar and prayer book in hand Page conducted the ceremony. There was no ring but the couple considered that they were truly married.

The diversion to Hooksway takes you past and the official route takes you close to Telegraph House. Telegraph House was originally one of the 10 signal stations were built in 1796 during the Napoleonic Wars to keep the Admiralty in London in communication with the fleet based at Portsmouth.

The system first used was a series of six shutters that could be opened and closed to give 64 combinations. That was the system that was in operation at date of the Battle of Trafalgar in 1805. It could get a short message to London in 7½ minutes although no doubt wordier messages took longer. This considerably beat the minimum time of 4½ hours that it took on horseback although the need for horseman did not disappear at night or when visibility was bad.

The shutter system was superseded in 1822 by a semaphore system that used moveable 'arms' with a chain of 15 stations and, although most of the original stations were not used, Telegraph House did remain in service until it was overtaken in 1847 by the then more cutting edge of technology with the coming of the railways and the introduction of the Electric Telegraph.

For those who use their mobile phones to send text messages, abbreviating words to save time, the Royal Navy was there over two hundred years ago. It was quite usual for similar abbreviations to be used in naval signals for the same reason.

A restored semaphore station can be seen at Chately Heath near Cobham in Surrey.

Back on the Way the church below the Downs with the green coloured, copper clad broach spire is St Mary and St Gabriel at South Harting.

South Harting was the place where the four companions of Belloc's book, **The Four Men**, parted: Grizzlebeard, the Poet, the Sailor and Myself. They had completed their 1902 crossing of Sussex from Robertsbridge in East Sussex, mainly on foot, singing, talking and drinking as they went. This was a journey the essence of which was recreated in 2003, the fiftieth anniversary of Belloc's death. In essence because Belloc's travellers walked mainly on the roads but the roads that they then walked are no longer safe for man or beast. Of the other elements, talk there was a plenty and an occasional voice was raised in song; the drinking is left to your imagination.

Just to the north west of South Harting is Torberry Hill which was formed by the spoon that the Devil flung aside in pain and rage after burning his lips on the steaming punch from his Punch Bowl in Surrey.

South Harting is also where the novelist Anthony Trollope (1815-1882) lived and wrote during the last two years of his life. He was a prodigious worker with an output that includes 47 novels as well as travel books, biographies, plays, short stories and literary sketches.

In spite of all that, for many years writing was not the day job. Trollope joined the General Post Office in London as junior clerk in 1834 at the age of 19. Over the years he made upwards progress. He travelled extensively for the Post Office, undertook missions to Egypt, the West Indies and the United States and introduced the pillar-box for letters to Great Britain. He retired in 1867 as a successful and important civil servant.

His literary career did not begin until 1847 with the publication of his first novel although success was to come later with the publication of **The Warden**, the first of the Barsetshire Chronicles. In the years that he was working for the Post Office he wrote a set number of words early in the morning before leaving for the office. He wrote when he was travelling by rail or sea and, as soon as he finished one novel, started another. Somehow amidst all this he was a hunting man to the point of obsession.

When you come over the final rise of Harting Down you can see a bare hill top ahead rising amongst the trees on which there are the remains of what is traditionally called the Vandalian Tower. The tower was built by Sir Matthew Featherstonhaugh (FANSHAW) of Uppark. Vandalia was to have been a colony in North America created by the American Grand Ohio Company in which Sir Matthew had invested in 1769. The scheme came to nothing due to the American War of Independence that broke out in 1775. It is more likely, however, that the tower was built as a banqueting room to celebrate the coming of age of Sir Matthew's son, Harry.

No doubt Harry, a noted rake of his day, would have put the banqueting room to good use but it does not provide shelter today for passers-by to eat their sandwiches. It not only is on private property, it is also in ruins. Apparently it was burnt by arsonists in 1842 in a troubled period when incendiarism was used as a means of protest against amendments to the Poor Law that agricultural labourers feared would cause loss of income.

Not long before the border with Hampshire and less than a mile to the south of the Way, but not visible from it, lies Uppark, risen like the Phoenix from the disastrous fire in 1989 when through the human chain formed by staff and visitors, 90% of the ground floor contents were saved.

There are two connections with the Napoleonic wars: one with the Army: the other with the Navy.

The house was offered to the Duke of Wellington as a reward for his services to the nation in the defeat of Napoleon. A price had been agreed but he, seeing its position at the top of a steep hill, calculated that the toll on his horseflesh would be too great. "*I have crossed the Alps once*", he said and accepted the offer of Stratfield Saye in Hampshire instead.

The naval connection is more tenuous. The rakish Sir Harry Featherstonhaugh inherited the house in 1774. For a while he kept a teenage mistress there who, it was said, danced on the tables in somewhat less that her crinoline. Her name was Emma Hart. After she and Sir Harry broke up she met, and later married, the British Ambassador to Naples. Naples was then a separate kingdom. He was Sir William Hamilton and on her marriage she became Lady Hamilton. She met Nelson and entered the history books.

Sir Harry later gave up his life of wine, women and song to retire to the peace of Uppark. The life must have suited him. In his 70s he married Mary Ann Bullock, his head dairy maid, who was considerably younger than he. He died aged 92. Mary Ann, followed by her sister Frances, lived on in the house until Frances died in 1892, both keeping the house as Sir Harry knew it and saving it from any 'improvements' that the Victorians might have wanted to make.

H G Wells (1866-1946) the novelist and science-fiction writer best known for **The War of the Worlds**, knew the house in the days of the sisters but from 'below stairs'. His mother was the housekeeper there. The house appears as "*Bladesover*" in his novel **Tono-Bungay** (1909).

And so we cross into Hampshire. Nor a border post: not a line: not a sign. There does not even appear to be a significant increase in the pig population. On the map in Belloc's **The Four Men** Hampshire is marked "*Hic Porci*" – Here be Hogs. The border is about 75 metres after a bridleway going off to the left and about 200 metres before reaching a minor road at Sunwood Farm – and, like the Meridian, that's the best that we can do for you.

And this is the way that the South Downs Way ended until it was extended to Winchester in 1989: not so much with a bang as a whimper. The official guide published by the H M Stationery in 1977:

"Just beyond the unmarked boundary the Way meets a surfaced road, which descends to the South Harting-Petersfield road. *Buses run from South Harting to Petersfield.*" (The guide's own italics)

The author does, however go on to say, "*Few people, I believe, will want to end the Way so indecisively*" and gives directions to reach Buriton. There could have been worse places to finish. Buriton is a pleasant, picturesque village where there are licensed premises and where Edward Gibbon (1737-1794), author of the six volumes of that truly monumental work **The Decline and Fall of the Roman Empire**, spent much of his youth. His father owned the Manor House next to the church. None of the book was written there but Gibbon was happy there. He wrote of the house, "*An old mansion in a state of decay has been converted into the fashion and convenience of a modern house, of which I occupied the most agreeable apartment, and if strangers had nothing to see, the inhabitants had nothing to desire*".

This stage finishes at the Queen Elizabeth Country Park. It was named in 1953 in honour of the present Queen's coronation in that year. It is jointly managed by Hampshire County Council and Forest Enterprise (the old Forestry Commission) and it covers 564 hectares (1,400 acres).

It is split in two by the A3, the Portsmouth road. On the nearer east side War Down and Holt Down are well wooded. There are beech trees on War Down but Holt Down with its deeper top soil has Western red cedar, Corsican pine and Western hemlock as well as the beech; quicker maturing they will be felled for timber long before the beech. Some of the beech may well still be here in 150 years time. The beech is the queen of trees but, best of all, a prayer said under a beech goes straight to heaven. And that is just what some of us may need for Butser Hill on the next stage.

Queen Elizabeth Park to Exton

"I in these flowery meads would be;
These crystal streams should solace me;
To whose harmonious bubbling noise,
I with my angle will rejoice;
Sit here, and see the turtle-dove
Court his chaste mate to acts of love."

Izaak Walton
(1593-1638)

From Queen Elizabeth Park, the Way passes under the A3, the Portsmouth Road, to ascend Butser Hill: not quite to the top but close enough. At 270 metres (889 feet) Butser Hill is the highest point of the South Downs and also in Hampshire. It is also the culmination of the main ridge of the Downs which become less pronounced as we move towards Winchester. The actual height climbed up from the Park is about 134 metres (440 feet).

Butser Hill is scattered with prehistoric remains: cross dykes, tumuli and field systems. At the top the cafe and toilet block is built in the form of an Iron Age roundhouse. A realistic example of a roundhouse can be seen at Butser Ancient Farm about a mile to the south of the Country Park at the foot of Windmill Hill at Chalton.

© Butser Ancient Farm

Founded in 1972 the Ancient Farm moved to its present site in 1991. It is a full scale working reproduction of an Iron Age farm from about 300 BC with buildings, animals and crops of the period. It does not, however, neglect technical advance. A Roman villa has recently been constructed complete with hypocaust (central heating system). The Farm is more than a museum. It is a laboratory too, using modern methods to investigate Iron Age and Roman life, agriculture and building techniques. The Farm is opened to the public but it would be wise to check opening days and hours on the Farm's website, *www.butser.org.uk*, before visiting.

Looking back from the top of Butser Hill, or more often on the way up for those of us who like to make close and regular inspections of the landscape as we go, there is a bird's eye view of the road. It was always an important road serving the great naval port of Portsmouth but it did have its drawbacks.

Samuel Pepys mentions the need of a guide from Gildford (sic) to Petersfield and, on another occasion, how they had to get a countryman to guide them to Havant to avoid going through the forest. There were also the attentions of the highwaymen; Claude Duval, Jerry Abershawe and Captain Jacques amongst others were likely to want to relieve you of your purse – if nothing more. It may not have been these here, the leading lights amongst their 'profession' with Duval, the gallant Frenchman known to dance a measure at the roadside with the wife of one of his victims, but there are records of Sir Simon Clarke, a baronet no less, who was caught and tried at Winchester. He was lucky; connections led to a pardon. Almost all who were caught were executed.

But speed was of the essence. There was a regular coach service between London and Portsmouth. It boasted, *"Ye Portsmouth Machine sets out from Ye Elephant and Castell and arrives presently by the Grace of God"*. Presently in this context meant two days at the least. The temptation is to make modern comparisons but the urge will be resisted and further comment avoided.

Charles Dickens also knew the road. He was born in Portsmouth. A little way south of the Country Park Centre the old road passes near Bottom Cottage which was once an inn. It was here *"yet twelve miles short"* of their destination that Nicholas Nickleby and Smike stopped on their weary way to Portsmouth seeking their fortunes. At the inn they fell in with Mr Vincent Crummles, the actor manager, and his troupe of travelling players. They shared his beef steak pudding, forsook their intention of taking ship at Portsmouth and for a while took up the strolling player's life instead.

The prominent chimney structure that will be seen well to the south during this stage is at the Fawley Oil Refinery close to Southampton. It is said that the chimney at 200 metres (656 feet) is the highest 'building' in the south of England overtopping the 175 metres (574 feet) of the Spinnaker Tower at Portsmouth finally opened in 2005. Although built, to many the chimney will not be considered to be a 'building'. Indeed, Chambers Dictionary (9th edition 2003) defines a building as *"a substantial structure for giving shelter, eg a house, office block"*. On safer ground is the claim that Fawley Refinery is one of the biggest machines in the UK. The same dictionary defines 'machine' as *"any artificial means or contrivance"* and the refinery falls well within that covering 3,250 acres (1,315 hectares), with over 330 giant tanks, towers taller than football pitches (not more than 130 yards (119m) and not less than 100 yards (91m)) and employing 1,400 people.

As a piece of incidental knowledge gathered in passing, a building is also a collective noun for a gathering of rooks.

Is it a peculiarly British habit to christen naval shore establishments, also known as 'stone frigates', with names as if they were ships even though they may be inland miles from the sea and would have great difficulty in proceeding in any direction other than down if they were on it? HMS Mercury that the Way passes is (or was) one of those. She, for such I suppose she must be called, was 'launched' during the Second World War and became the Navy's main signal school for communications and electronic warfare with up to 500 naval personnel under instruction at any one time. She is no longer in use.

The Sustainability Centre is immediately opposite HMS Mercury. It was set up by Earthworks Trust Ltd., a registered charity, formed to assist the development of more sustainable styles of living and working. The South Downs Natural Burial Site is on the 55 acre site where broadleaf woodland is being restored in place of conifers. The positions of the graves are carefully recorded but there are no headstones or permanent memorials to intrude.

But the Way lies onwards and, if going westward in the direction of Winchester, do take care to turn right along the Way at the end of HMS Mercury's fencing. Do not continue along the road. The turning is very easy to miss.

The prominent church with the grey broach spire that can be seen the foot of the Downs is All Saints at East Meon: grey because it is covered in lead.

In another of those almost imperceptible changes of landscape character that occur along the Downs, the Way passes through the Meon Springs Fly Fishery just before reaching Whitewool Farm. The waters from the springs flow northwards to join the River Meon near West Meon. The Meon, one of those clear chalk streams for which Hampshire is justifiably famous, rises just over a mile (2 kilometres) to the south of East Meon. It passes through that village before circling to the north through West Meon and then turning south through Wanford and Exton, the stopping place for this stage, where it will be met again.

The springs for a while give a unique and tranquil perspective to the Way and endorse Izaak Walton's words that if he *"might be judge, God never did make a more calm, quiet, innocent recreation than angling"*.

Care again needs to be taken in following the route when reaching the road after climbing out of the valley from Whitewool Farm and it is worth remembering here, and towards the end of this section, that it is not wise blithely to follow those in front. Turn left to walk beside the road. Although the official route of the South Downs Way runs along the road for 750 metres (820 yards) an alternative, and surely one of which even the most pure of the purists cannot complain, is after about 275 metres (300 yards) to enter the first car park of the Nature Reserve. Ignore the gate to the left immediately at the entrance to the car park. Go fully into the car park and then take a gate to the left and, at first maintaining the direction of the road, follow the edge of the ridge to curve round to the Iron Age Fort on top of Old Winchester Hill.

Old Winchester Hill, which now is taken to include not only the hill on which the Iron Age fort sits, but also the whole of the area covered by the National Nature Reserve, is one of those is cared for by English Nature to conserve wildlife and landscape. As far as possible sheep are used to maintain the grass, sometimes assisted by cattle, but the hand of man also has to intervene to clear the scrub that is beyond the capabilities of the animals and would otherwise choke the 'natural' landscape. The Reserve is consequently rich in animal and plant life, including some 37 species of butterfly, and, in July, although in Hampshire, the bright blue of the round-headed rampion, the emblem of the South Downs Society and known as the Pride of Sussex, but now much rarer there.

An English Nature leaflet that can be obtained near the car park will tell you much more including that juniper bushes also grow there and that their scented berries were once used to flavour gin. What it does not tell you how useful a juniper is at the front door. A witch is forced to count the multitude of tiny leaves before she can enter and, as it takes so long, she may lose interest and move on. It is also useful as a tonic to ensure your mare's pregnancy following a visit from the stallion: presumably without the gin.

At the Iron Age fort with its attendant selection of earlier Bronze Age barrows there is one of those ever useful toposcopes that can solve most arguments about what is where and how far away it is in the sweeping views that can be seen from the top of the hill; "almost" of course because there can be times when it is difficult enough to see the toposcope let alone the views that it unravels.

After coming down from Old Winchester Hill it is necessary to keep a sharp eye open for the waymarks for the South Downs Way as it crosses a disused railway in a belt of woodland.

Not long after that and just before reaching Exton the Way crosses the Meon. Although he does not specifically mention it in **The Compleat Angler,** Izaak Walton knew the river well. His daughter Ann married the Rector of Droxford, a bare two miles downstream from Exton, and he spent much of his later life there. The river must have been to the front of his mind when writing that Hampshire exceeded *"all England for swift, shallow, clear, pleasant brooks and store of Troutes"*.

Broadhalfpenny Down is a mile and a half south of HMS Mercury. That is where the Hambledon Club, formed in about 1750, played cricket and Hambledon, a village two miles further on, has been called 'The Cradle of Cricket'. It's not that cricket was invented there. Cricket must have been played in some form or another ever since man, and I use that word advisedly, found that he could derive equal pleasure from using his club to hit a round object rather than his neighbour – a conclusion that some alleged football supporters have yet to reach.

But Hambledon was where rules were formulated that became generally accepted and formed the foundation of the modern game.

And the men of Hambledon were invincible in their day. They frequently met and defeated All England sides. Their most famous victory was at Sevenoaks in 1777 when they beat All England by an innings and 168 runs and took home the purse of 1,000 guineas. There was big money in the game in those days and betting on the match results, so recently in the headlines, is nothing new.

Hambledon's position as the regulating authority of the game declined and disappeared with the formation of the MCC (Marylebone Cricket Club) in 1787 but, in a minor turn of a circle, the MCC played at Lord's Cricket Ground that became its home: Lord's Cricket Ground was founded by Thomas Lord also in 1787: and Thomas Lord, originally a Yorkshireman, is buried in the churchyard at West Meon where he died in 1832 having retired there to farm.

Exton to Winchester

"... an exceedingly pleasant Town, enriched with a beautiful Cathedral and surrounded by fresh-looking country."

John Keats
1819

Not long after the climb out of Exton, and immediately past Lomer Cottage, the site of the medieval village of Lomer lies on the left hand side of the Way. It is a mainly level area with a few low mounds in the grass: the biggest being said to be the church.

Lomer is one of those places that really are mentioned in the Domesday Book when it belonged to the Abbey of St Peters in Winchester.

There was no dramatic end for Lomer. It was not a casualty of war or of the plague but of economic forces brought about by agricultural enclosures and clearances in the valley: more common but less impressive reasons for villages being deserted.

The remains are not prominent. Stone, brick or substantial oak timber framing were not for the ordinary villager. Wooden huts or wattle and daub between posts sunk into the ground were the norm. These did not have long lives. The site is another of those reminders scattered throughout the Downs of people, now long forgotten, who once lived and worked where almost nothing remains.

Those who have been studying their maps may have noticed that just to the south west of Lomer Farm, and not the subject for schoolboy humour, is Betty Mundy's Bottom. In the Sussex dialect, 'Bottom', when it appears on a map of the Downs, means, simply, a valley in the Downs. The same applies in Hampshire and further along to the west in Dorset too. But who was Betty Mundy and why is Sailor's Wood at one end of her valley and Sargeant's Copse at the other?

The story goes, and no guarantee is given as to its authenticity, that, contrary to the strictures of aged parents to beware the perils of fast women and slow horses, many a serviceman, pockets awash with accumulated pay was lured to this place to sample the delights of Betty Mundy. It is best to draw a veil over whether they reached those arms or, indeed, if those arms existed at all, for this is a moral tale: most of the potential customers were relieved of their money and some of their lives too, being buried in the woods where their bodies were later found. It would be idle to speculate whether there was strict segregation, depending on the branch of the service, between burial in the Wood and the Copse – sergeants to the left and sailors to the right.

Those who have walked the coastal path in Dorset may know that the quarrymen of Purbeck were not so restrained in their sense of humour. Scratchy Bottom is close to Durdle Door and that is as far as the Ordnance Survey would permit local names to go on its maps.

The Milbury's is always a welcome sight whichever way you are travelling along the South Downs Way. If you count on your fingers, it is one of less than one handful of public houses that stand on the Way. Once the Fox and Hounds, it is now The Milbury's after the mill barrows, the barrows close by where the windmill stood.

The late, great Bob Copper MBE (1915-2005) was a man of many parts not least of which were writer and singer; and he was going to be mentioned come what may. For many of us he is synonymous with Sussex but he was no stranger to Hampshire where he collected the old songs and for a while was the landlord of the H H Inn (Hampshire Hunt) at Cheriton about 2½ miles northwards. In his book **Songs & Southern Breezes** (1973), he described that part of Beauworth where The Milbury's lies as "…*one of those rare places in southern England that can boast a school and a pub but has no church. So, while its children's thirst for knowledge and the arid throats of its menfolk can be quenched at the abundant and never-failing fountains of the village school or the Fox and Hounds, those good souls who thirst after more spiritual refreshment remain parched or walk the mile and a half down the road into the village proper*".

He also tells stories of Jim Wicks whose "*antediluvian tricycle … seemed to have a homing instinct directed on the great beech tree that stood outside the Fox and Hounds*", and of John Hoare, the sometime landlord, who doubled as the village carpenter and wheelwright, who lovingly fashioned his own coffin that was an object for the admiration of those who were given a tour of the inn. But these stories are better told by Bob.

The inn has what was once one of the essentials for survival on the Downs, its own supply of water. Not one of Bob Copper's fountains but a well of very respectable depth, some 300 feet. Do not look for it outside. It is inside the pub. A donation will secure a glass full of ice cubes that can be sent plummeting one by one until delayed splashes record their arrival down below.

The well was man powered. In Bob Copper's book there is a photograph of Fred Hoare, John's son, standing upright in the 12 foot diameter treadmill, his head about level with the bottom of the great axle. The author was greatly tempted, purely in the interests of research, to try the wheel when the staff were distracted elsewhere but this would not have justified the possible destruction of a 250 year old artefact no matter how well intentioned.

There are not too many choices of continuous routes from east to west in Sussex. In the south there is the A and M27 and there is the South Downs Way if you walk or ride, be it horse or bicycle. There is also the A272, the road that has an ode written to it: Pieter Boogaarts' **A272: An Ode to a Road** first published in 2000. Both the A272 and the Way start in East Sussex within a few degrees of longitude gradually converging as they both head for Winchester, the road shadowing the South Downs in their later stages until both road and Way meet; first when the Way crosses the road at Holden Farm and then when the Way re-crosses the road some two miles further along the road at Cheesefoot Head. Here a finger post at the roadside shows that Exton is 8½ miles behind and Winchester but 3½ miles ahead.

There is a natural amphitheatre just below Cheesefoot Head. It is known locally as the Devil's Punch Bowl but should not be confused with the better known Punch Bowl in Surrey. It was here that General Eisenhower is said to have addressed the allied troops immediately before the invasion of Normandy on D Day, 6th June 1944. As we know, the South Downs were very much an armed camp during the Second World War and it could have been on this occasion that Eisenhower described the Downs as part of "*a great human spring, coiled for the moment when its energy should be released and it would vault the English Channel in the greatest amphibious assault ever attempted*". The great Joe Louis, heavyweight world champion, topped the bill here at a boxing tournament organised for the troops about 6 weeks before D Day. It is now used for concerts.

Cheesefoot Head is also well known to cerealogists for many an agriglyph has been seen there. Cerealogy (sometimes rendered cereology) is the study of crop circles and agriglyphs are the crop circles themselves. Crop circles have engaged the public from about 1980 appearing, it would seem, with greater frequency and in increasingly complex patterns.

In his book Pieter Boogaart mentions that Cheesefoot Head was the first place that they were seen and, in a way, he may be right for two very terrestrial circle makers have admitted to making circles there in 1978. Circles had, however, been reported in various places prior to that: England in the 1930s and 1940s: France in 1954: Australia in 1966. But these did not then engage the public attention. It is also claimed that references to crop circles in England go back to the 16th and 17th centuries. It remains to be seen whether they are a hoax, the result of meteorological conditions or extraterrestrial intervention, especially as the complexity of pattern seems to rule out all but the latter. The message *"Tis for England"* that Pieter Boogaart reports as having seen in 1995 requesting that Matthew Le Tisier of Southampton be picked for the national football side does provide compelling evidence of an alien intelligence at work.

The change in the landscape character in the Downs towards the end of the Way can clearly be seen from Cheesefoot Head. The underlying chalk that produces the rounded contours of the hill is still there but, here in Hampshire, the landscape is dominated by a few individual hills. There are Butser Hill, Old Winchester Hill and Beacon Hill above Exton but the Downs are more open with longer sweeping views and fewer hedgerows.

Once the A272 has been crossed at Cheesefoot Head, walk ahead along the Way for 200 metres and follow it as it turns right. It soon enters a narrow patch of scrub. On emerging, all being well with the weather, over to the left there are the first signs of Winchester from its higher sited buildings. On emerging from the second patch there are views down into the centre of the city. It is difficult to identify the individual buildings, particularly if you do not know the city well. Unlike Chichester the cathedral is not immediately apparent. Its tower is not tall and does not dominate its surroundings like the spire of Chichester Cathedral over the Sussex Coastal Plain. But the end of the journey is in sight.

A mile or so short of Winchester, some modernistic buildings have appeared to the north below the ridge of the Downs with a large satellite dish in close attendance. They are nothing to with crop circles and the dish is not to improve the reception of Sky Television but belongs to a telephone company, NTL. The remainder of the site is occupied by INTECH.

Run by the Hampshire Technology Centre Trust Ltd., an educational charity, INTECH seeks to provide a *"true 'hands-on' learning experience"* for all ages in science, technology, engineering and mathematics with a range of displays and interactive exhibits. An ecology study centre is also planned where natural life can be observed as the site, in the words of the publicity leaflet, *"settles back into its Downland setting"*.

Winchester to the Romans was Venta Belgarum, the town of the Belgii, the local Celtic tribe who were in residence when the Romans arrived, possibly not as unwelcome visitors; they seem to have arrived in the south more by invitation than as conquerors. The serious fighting was later. What was to become Winchester was already a place of settlement when the Romans came and laid out their chequerboard pattern of streets that is still reflected in the street pattern of the town today.

Others that we have encountered on the way are there before us. The body of King Ethelwulf, the father of Alfred the Great was moved here from Steyning, Izaak Walton is buried in the cathedral and King Alfred the Great (849-899), who we left possibly burning the cakes at Alfriston, was also buried in Winchester. He was first buried in the Old Minster that stood where the Cathedral now stands but his remains were moved several times before being buried in front of the high altar of the church of Hyde Abbey some way to the north of the cathedral. That church was demolished during the Reformation in the 16th century and the site of the grave unmarked and forgotten. The site has been rediscovered but there are no longer any remains there. They were probably discarded in 1788 when the area was being cleared by prisoners for the County gaol but Alfred's greatness lives on.

The fortunes of Winchester declined after rule from Rome ended in Britain but were revived under Alfred the Great when it became the capital of England. In later centuries this was jointly with London until the 12th century when, with growing centralisation – even in those days – London became the sole capital, although even as late as the 17th century Charles II had plans to build a palace there. Designed by Sir Christopher Wren, it would have rivalled Versailles.

Having crossed the motorway (M3) there is little to show the route into the heart of Winchester. Essentially one turns right at the end of the motorway bridge for 250 metres (275 yards) and then left to follow the road for about a kilometre (1100 yards). Where East Hill meets Chesil Street near the pub, The Blackboy, cross the road by the pedestrian crossing and then, if on foot, a quick left and right to maintain the direction down to the Itchen, one of those Hampshire chalk streams and the last of the six rivers to cross. One can turn right along Chesil Street to the High Street but the foregoing is the more scenic route.

If one has chosen the scenic route, turn right alongside the Itchen and follow the river until it brings you to the High Street. Here turn left to the great statue of Alfred, sword raised on high. The statue is by Hamo Thornycroft and was erected in the Broadway in 1901 to mark Alfred's millennium. It is a fitting if not the official end.

Winchester was not only politically important. It was also a centre of ecclesiastical power with bishop and cathedral. The present cathedral may have a tower that is only 140 feet tall but it is said (at 556 feet) to be the longest Gothic cathedral in the world. The word 'Gothic' must be emphasised. The claim to be the longest cathedral in the world lies elsewhere.

Winchester Cathedral must be one of the few ecclesiastical buildings, if not the only one, to be celebrated in the popular culture of more recent years. At the mention of Winchester Cathedral a tune will immediately come to mind for most of the generation that grew up in the 1960s, who are a bit greyer now, and maybe a few before and since as well. But who were responsible?

It is almost an accident that never happened. The song was written by Geoff Stephens who hired a group of session musicians to record it. The record was released in 1966. **Winchester Cathedral** became a great hit, achieving Number 1 in the USA. After that a band that did not exist was expected to go on tour. A band was hurriedly assembled. Alan Klein, who had not been on the original recording, was the vocalist and dubbed the seventh Earl of Cricklewood. The band was the New Vaudeville Band and there were a few more hits. Some of us can still recall the delights of **Finchley Central**.

Winchester was also a place of pilgrimage and a place on the way of pilgrimages. It had its own saint, St Swithun, who may be familiar as the harbinger of rain. One version of the old rhyme goes:

> *"St Swithun's Day, if thou dost rain*
> *Full forty days it will remain,*
> *St Swithun's Day, if thou be fair*
> *For forty days , 'twill rain no mair."*

Under the modern calendar, St Swithun's Day is 15 July.

Not a lot is known about St Swithun. He was bishop of Winchester, then a very important bishopric, from 852 AD until his death in 862. He may have been tutor to King Ethelwulf, King Alfred's father, and may have been accompanied Alfred on a pilgrimage to Rome before Alfred became king.

The legend is that St Swithun, who was Bishop of Winchester but a holy and humble man, wished to be buried in the churchyard so that the *"sweet rain of heaven might fall upon his grave"*. That was done but, a 100 years later, he was to be canonised and it was felt more fitting that the body of a saint should be removed from the lowly churchyard to a shrine in the cathedral itself. The heavens replied with 40 days of continuous rain to express his sadness and that delayed his removal into the cathedral for that long.

The pilgrimages were a two way traffic. Winchester was on the way in and also on the way out. Pilgrims came in from the mainland of Europe to the English shrines; St Swithun himself: Walsingham in Norfolk known as England's Nazareth: and, later, Canterbury, where Thomas à Becket was murdered in 1170.

And, in the other direction, after paying one's respects to St Swithun, one took ship at Portsmouth and made one's way to the major shrines of western Christendom probably via Mont St Michel in Normandy.

To adopt the speak of the time (according to Dante), the Palmers went to the Holy Land, the Romei to Rome, and the Pilgrims to St Iago de Compostela in northern Spain. Compostela was, and still is, the shrine of St James the Greater – St Iago Matamoros – the slayer of the Moors. He provided the symbol for reconquest of Spain from the Moors as evidenced by the exploits of Rodrigo Diaz de Vivar (1043-1099) – El Cid – also known as Charlton Heston. But, perhaps, it should be remembered that he who conquers writes the history and Hollywood can turn it into fact.

There are ways to follow beyond. Hampshire County Council has developed two waymarked trails from Winchester. Going south there are the 28 miles of the Pilgrims' Trail to Portsmouth. From there the really intrepid, following the example of ages past, might cross the Channel and find their way down through France past Mont St Michel to join up with one of the main pilgrim routes to Compostela. To the north east there is the 34 mile St Swithun's Trail to Farnham where it joins the Pilgrim's Way to Canterbury.

And there is always the Way back to Eastbourne.

A Postscript

"Above all do not lose your desire to walk: every day I walk myself into a state of well-being and walk away from every illness; I have walked myself into my best thoughts, and I know of no thought so burdensome that one cannot walk away from it."

Søren Kierkegaard

And Where Do We Go From Here?

Some further reading:

The written sources that have been consulted have been many and varied but only a selection of those will be listed here some of which have already been mentioned in the text. Some are currently not in print but should be available at the public library (in Sussex at least). If, like me, you are a fervent hoarder of books it should be possible to obtain copies through the Internet from Amazon or Abebooks.

The dates given are those of the first publication to give an idea of time scale but some were reprinted and the reprints can give good reading copies, probably at a lower cost, if you are interested in buying. The older books that I know to have been reissued have been marked with an asterisk*.

For an overall view of the South Downs that it would be difficult to better and not for many, many years:
The South Downs: Peter Brandon (1998)

For general views but not as comprehensive or up to date as Dr. Brandon:
Along the South Downs: David Harrison (1958)
The South Downs: Ben Darby (1976)

For the wildlife:
Unto the Hills: Patrick Coulcher (2001)

For the Downs as they were and life on them as it was:
Nature in Downland: W H Hudson (1900 but paperback published in 1981)
The Spirit of the Downs: Arthur Beckett (1909 but 7 editions the last in 1944)
Shepherds of Sussex: Barclay Wills (1938)*
A South Down Farm in the 1860s: Maude Robinson (1938)*

And, without disrespect to Paul Millmore, Kev Reynolds, the South Downs Society or any others who have described the South Downs Way more recently, my favourite guide:
A guide to the South Downs Way: Miles Jebb (1984)
Now out of print and out of date in some ways it still is worth looking at. I have had my own copy since 1984 but have bought copies for others far more recently and very reasonably from second hand book shops. I also know that Horsham Library has a copy on its shelves.

Acknowledgements

One realises well before one sits back at the last word with a smug smile of self satisfaction on one's face and a feeling of euphoria that lasts a brief moment before doubt comes crashing in how many have helped to unravel some of the more tricky problems or, indeed, to verify a passing reference. If I got the answer right it is due to them and, let us be charitable, if I got it wrong, it was a misunderstanding on my part at worst, though some might say otherwise. Amongst those to whom my gratitude is due, and some of them may be surprised to find themselves in this list, and may wish that they were not, are Nick Birkett of the National Trust, John Brough who drove those Churchill tanks in World War II, Butser Ancient Farm, Simon Culpin of what is now the South Downs Joint Committee, Brenda Lorkin-Goodman, Bridget Rose for her continual guidance on design, E J who slew the computer dragons, Vivien Lyth and Keith McKenna of Footprints, the network (or is it Mafia) of Parish Clerks of which I was a member until recently including Ingrid Caygill at Upper Beeding and Philip Ayers at Cuckmere Valley, Dave Pearce the Downland Ranger for Eastbourne Borough Council, the Samaritans at Eastbourne, the Visitor Centre at Exceat and the West Sussex Library Service particularly at Horsham.

We sincerely hope that there are none that have been unwittingly overlooked: our apologies and thanks also to any that there may be.